The Snowflake Making Guide: 25 Easy Fold Templates

ELLA BRETT-TURNER, CREATOR OF SNOWFLAKES OF TIKTOK

The Snowflake Making Guide

www.instagram.com/snowflakesoftiktok/

ISBN: 979-8-218-29983-5

DEDICATION

To my Uncle Phil. Unique, even for snowflakes.

CONTENTS

ACKNOWLEDGMENTS

Thank you to my Mom, who contributed her photo-editing skills and expertise. Without her precise editing and no-shortcuts approach, this book would not have been possible. Lastly, thank you to my followers, friends and family who supported me along the way. I am excited to share this book with you.

INTRODUCTION

Dear fellow Snowflake-Maker,

Thank you for purchasing this book! After a year of sharing my love of snowflake-making online via @snowflakesoftiktok, I wanted to share my designs and techniques in print.

I started making snowflakes a few months after graduating from university. After many years of studying, making snowflakes reminded me how much I missed art class.

Adults often don't have time to or are not encouraged to create. For me, making snowflakes is a way to make art (and messes) in a way I have not done since I was a small child. I hope this book helps you to do the same.

Let's get started!

HOW TO USE THIS BOOK

This book is a guide to help you make your own snowflakes. Here is how to use this book:

- Start by cutting out a template from the TEMPLATE section on page 11. They will work best if you trim them using the black square as a guide. The templates are in order from easiest to hardest. Try starting with one of the easier templates!

- Next, go to the HOW TO FOLD THE PAPER FOR SNOWFLAKES section on page 5. Follow the step-by-step instructions to fold and cut your snowflake.

- Check out the TIPS AND TRICKS FOR FOLDING AND CUTTING section on page 9 to improve your snowflake-making technique.

- Work your way through the templates from beginner to advanced to build up your skills. If you want to repeat any snowflake, you can always fold your own sheet of paper and trace one of the designs from the APPENDIX on page 87.

- When you're comfortable cutting out the templates, read the DESIGNING YOUR OWN SNOWFLAKES section. Use the templates from the BLANK TEMPLATES section on page 71 to draw and cut your own designs.

- Now that you have a collection of snowflakes, try some of the ideas to display them in DISPLAYING YOUR SNOWFLAKES on page 81.

Let's make some snowflakes!

How to fold the paper for snowflakes

YOU WILL NEED:

One template

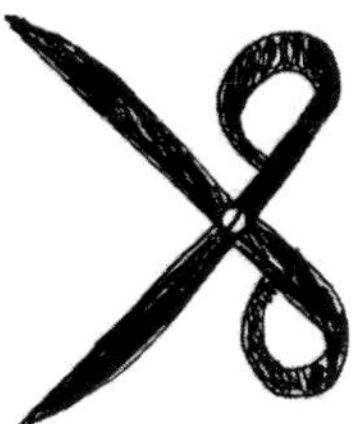

Scissors

STEP ONE

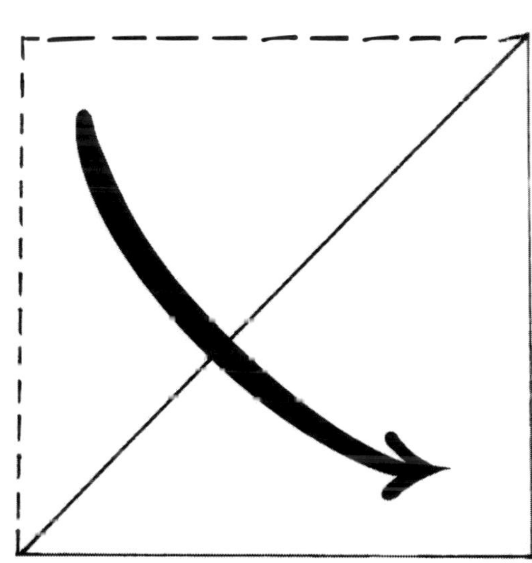

Fold corners
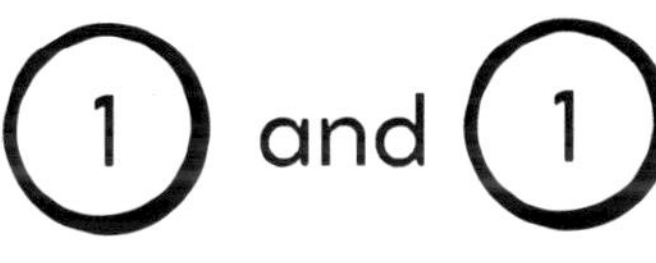

to meet.

Fold along the solid black line.

Now the square is folded in half diagonally.

STEP TWO

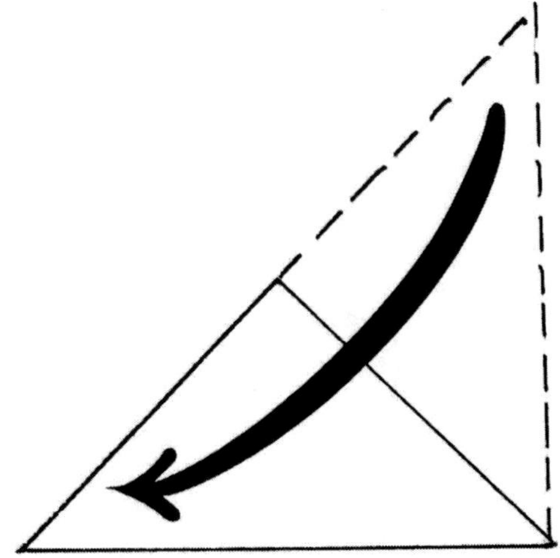

Fold corners (2) and (2) to meet.

Now the paper is folded in quarters diagonally.

STEP THREE

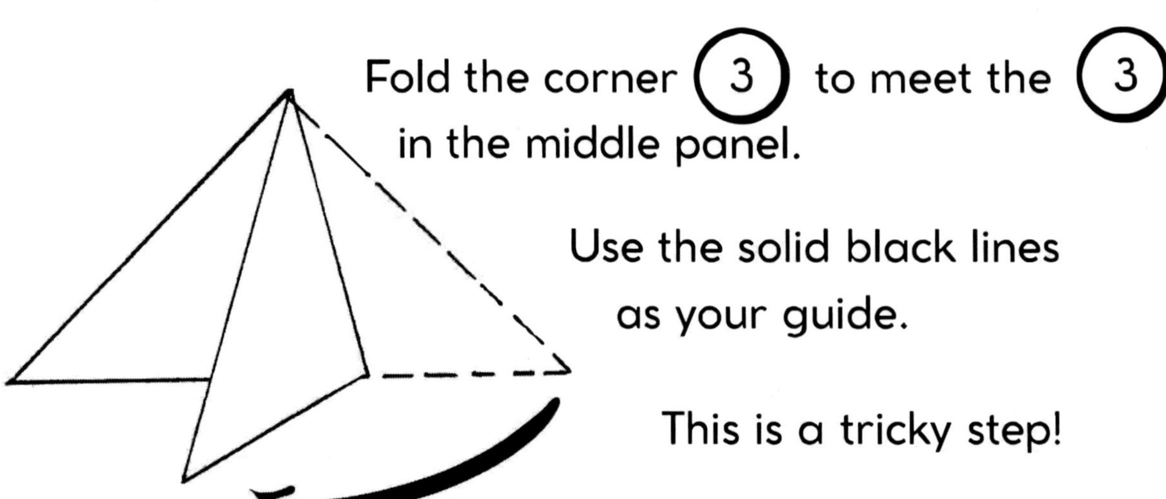

Fold the corner (3) to meet the (3) in the middle panel.

Use the solid black lines as your guide.

This is a tricky step!

We are folding the triangle into thirds.

This way our final snowflake will have twelve panels.

STEP FOUR:

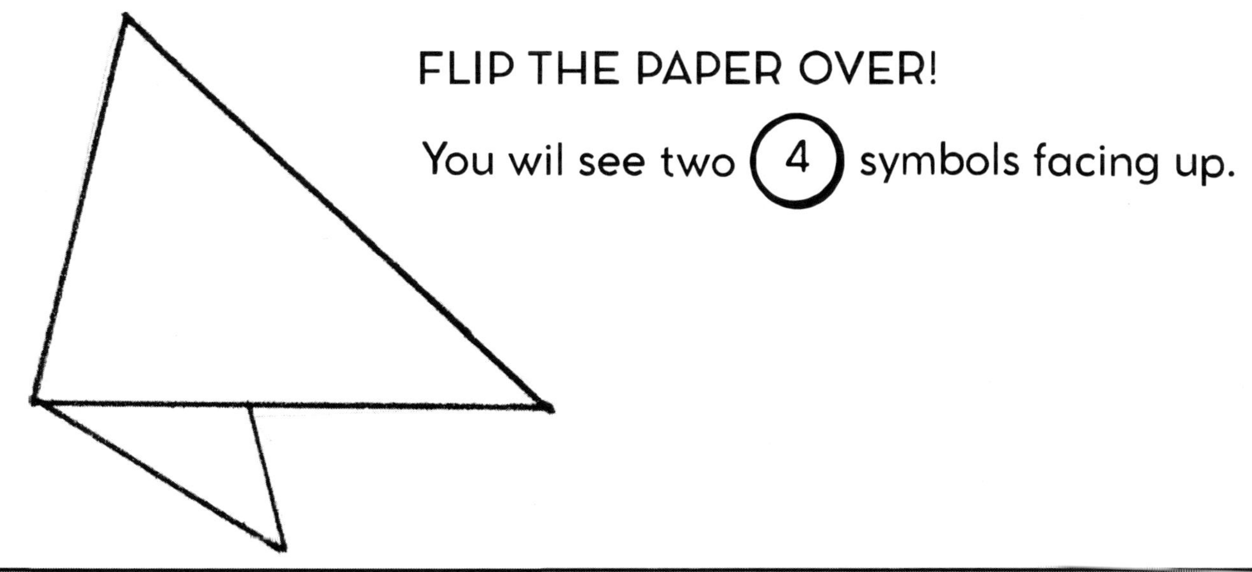

FLIP THE PAPER OVER!

You wil see two (4) symbols facing up.

STEP FIVE:

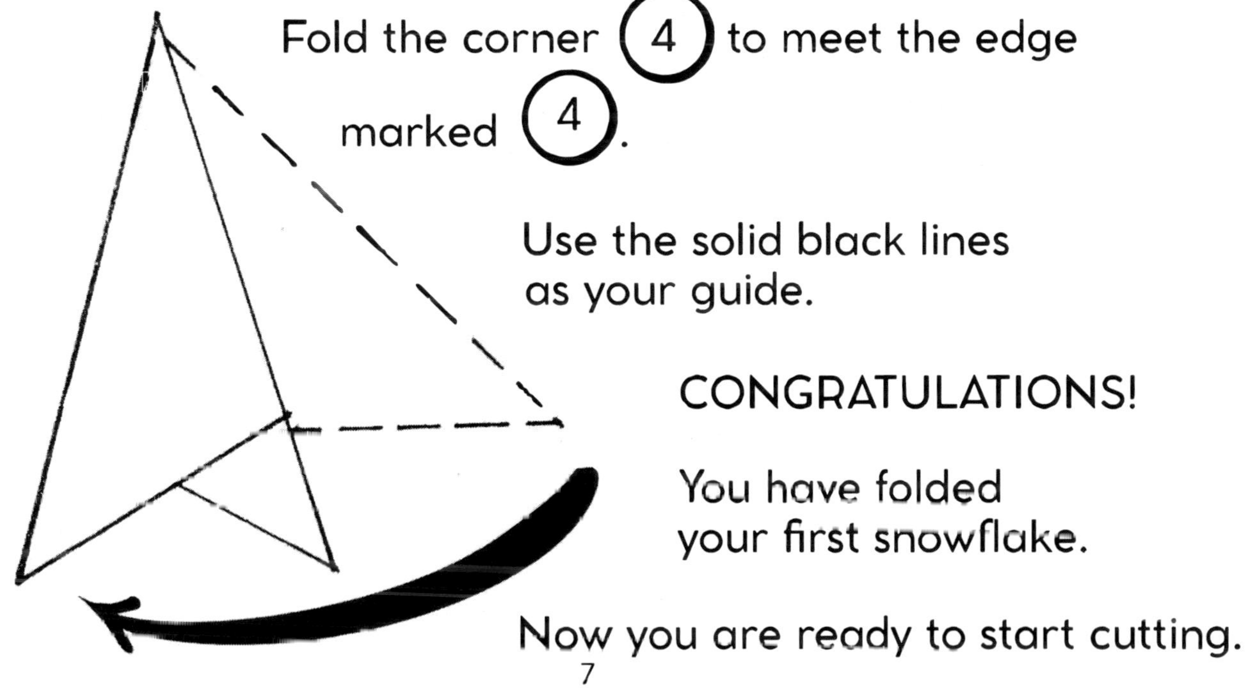

Fold the corner (4) to meet the edge marked (4).

Use the solid black lines as your guide.

CONGRATULATIONS!

You have folded your first snowflake.

Now you are ready to start cutting.

STEP SIX

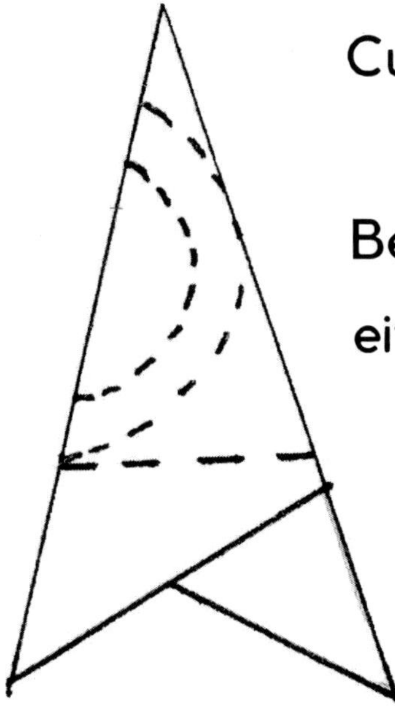

Cut along the dotted black lines.

Be careful not to cut through either side completely.

STEP SEVEN

UNFOLD!

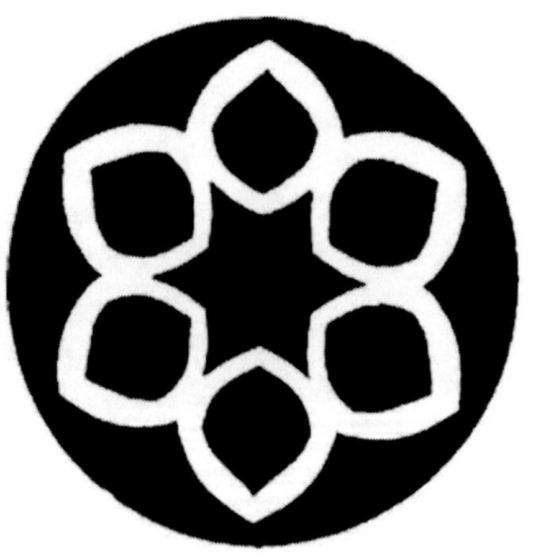

TIPS AND TRICKS FOR FOLDING AND CUTTING

- **Try to fold as precisely as possible!** The more precise your folds are, the more symmetrical your snowflake will be.
- **Use the black lines as a guide for your folds.**
- **Use a ruler to press down your folds.**

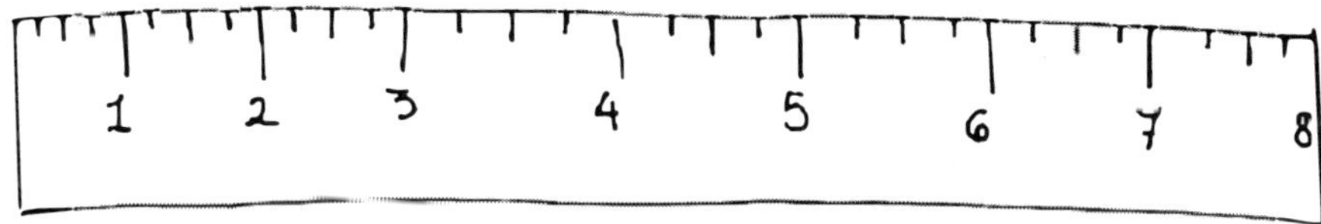

- **Sharp scissors are best.** Try using a few different sizes of scissors to cut out different shapes.

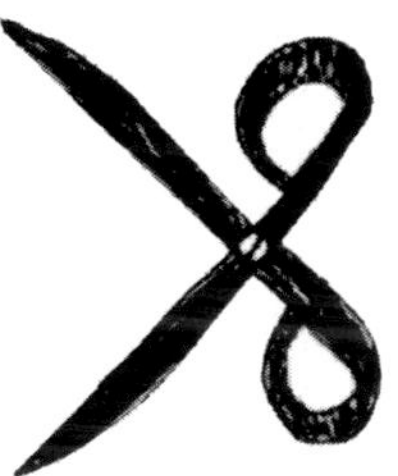

- **Cut out fine details first.** Then, make larger cuts.
- **Hold the snowflake together tightly as you cut.**

- **Err on the side of caution!** It's easy to cut away more later, but hard to add paper back.
- **Unfold your snowflakes carefully!** Sometimes they stick to themselves and rip.

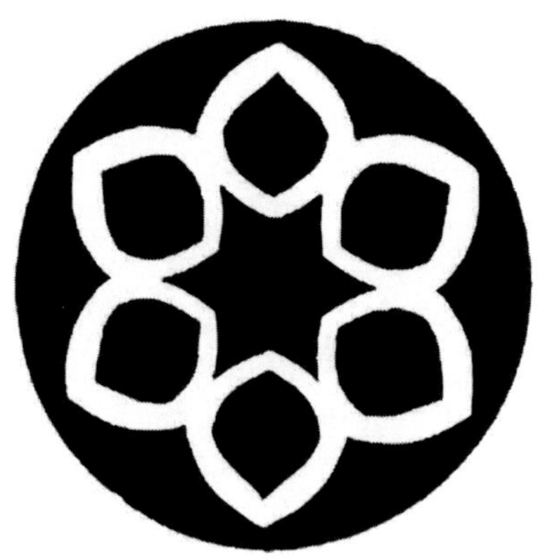

TEMPLATES

Please trim the templates to a square using the black square as your guide. Use the HOW TO FOLD THE PAPER FOR SNOWFLAKES instructions on page 5. If you make a mistake, the template designs are in the APPENDIX on page 85.

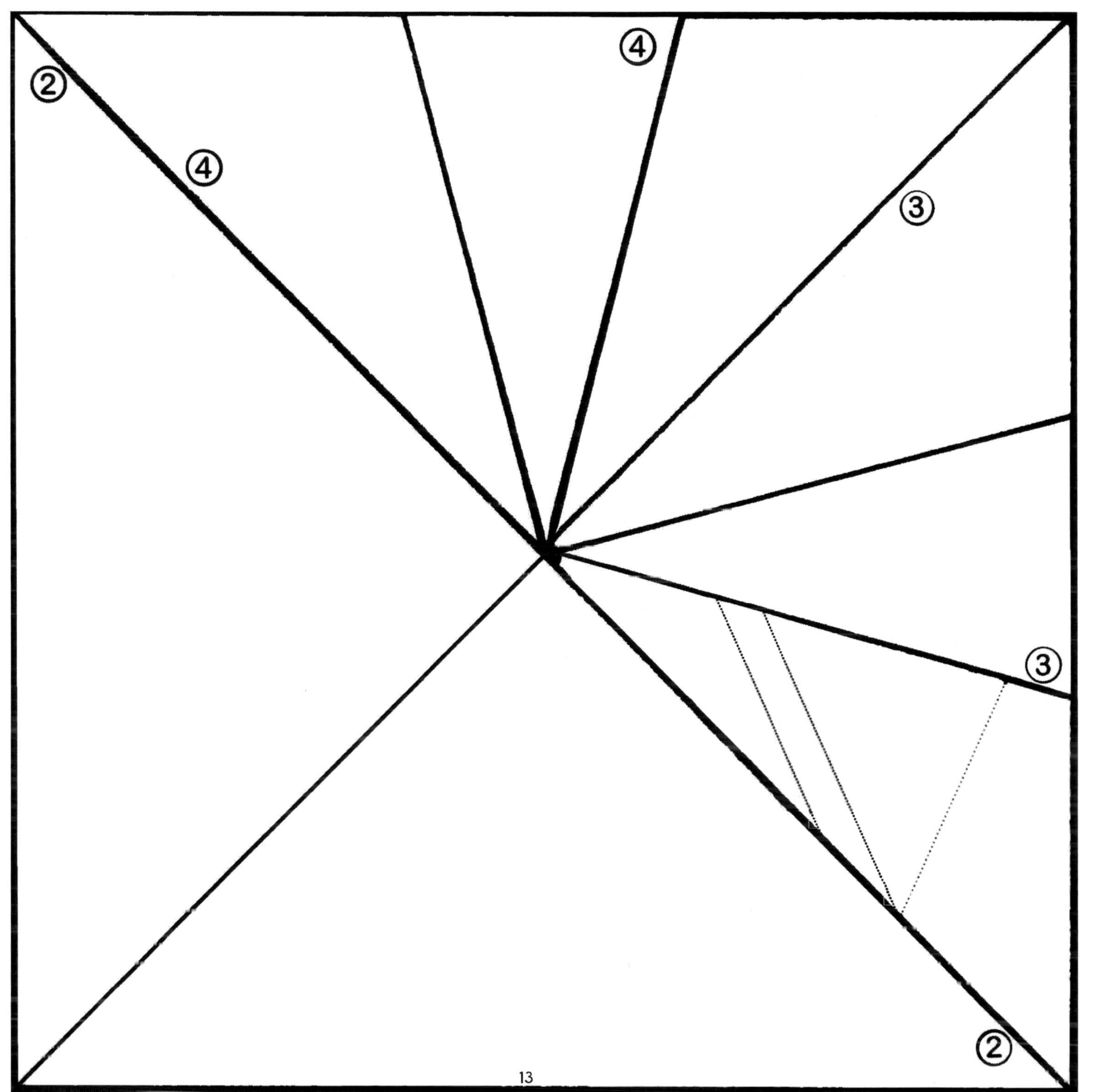
②
④
④
③
③
②

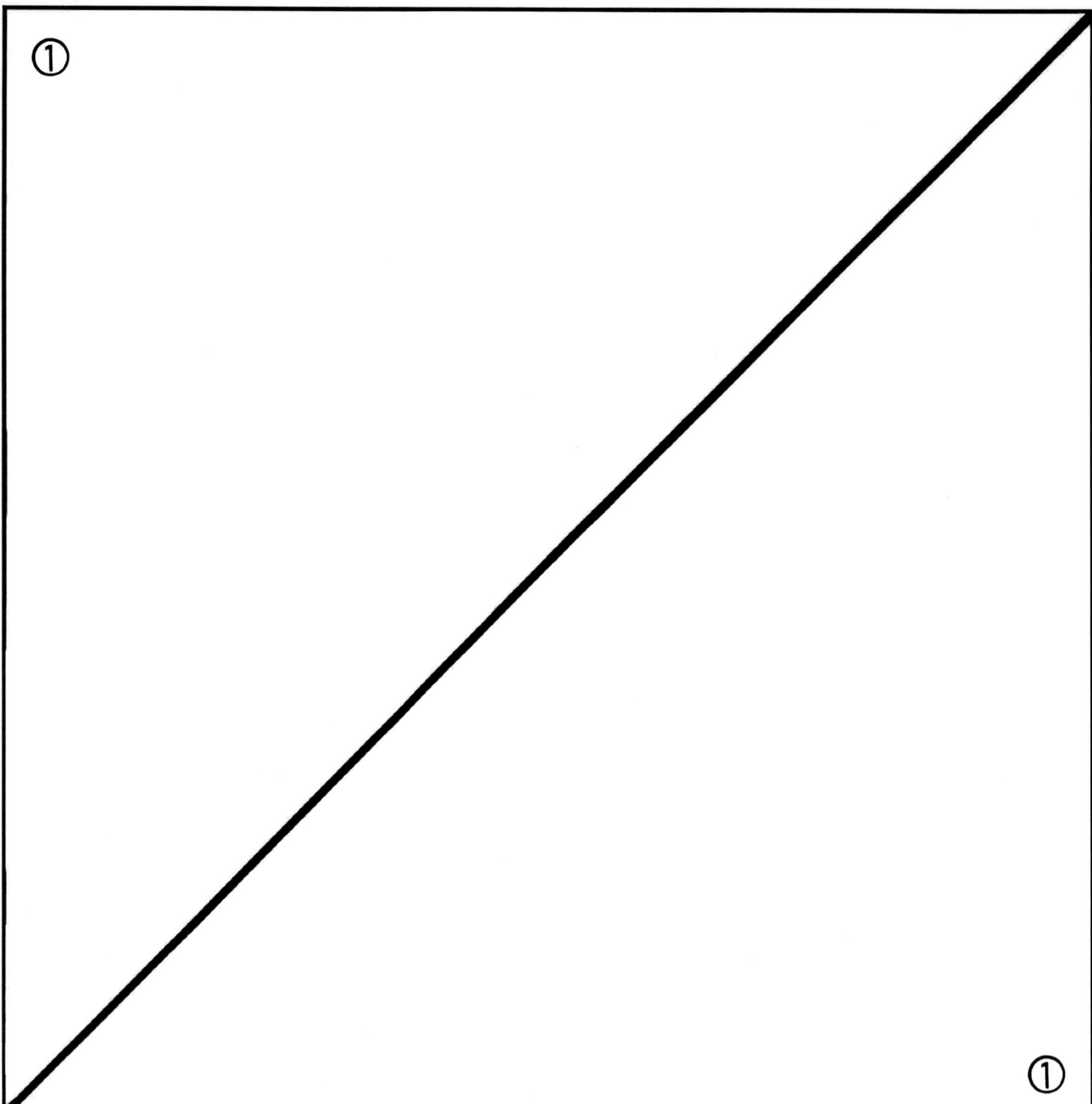
①
①

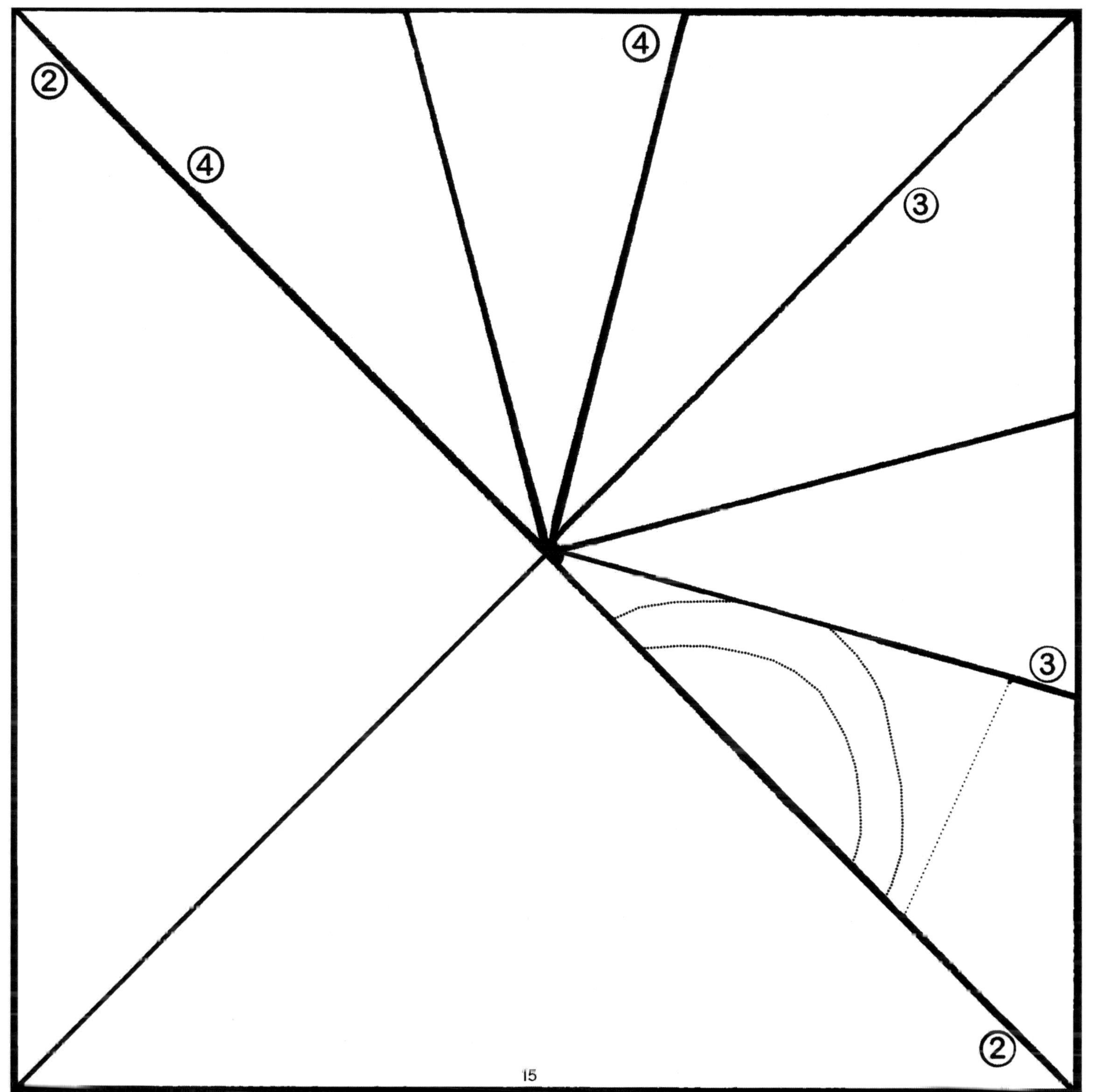
②
④
④
③
③
②

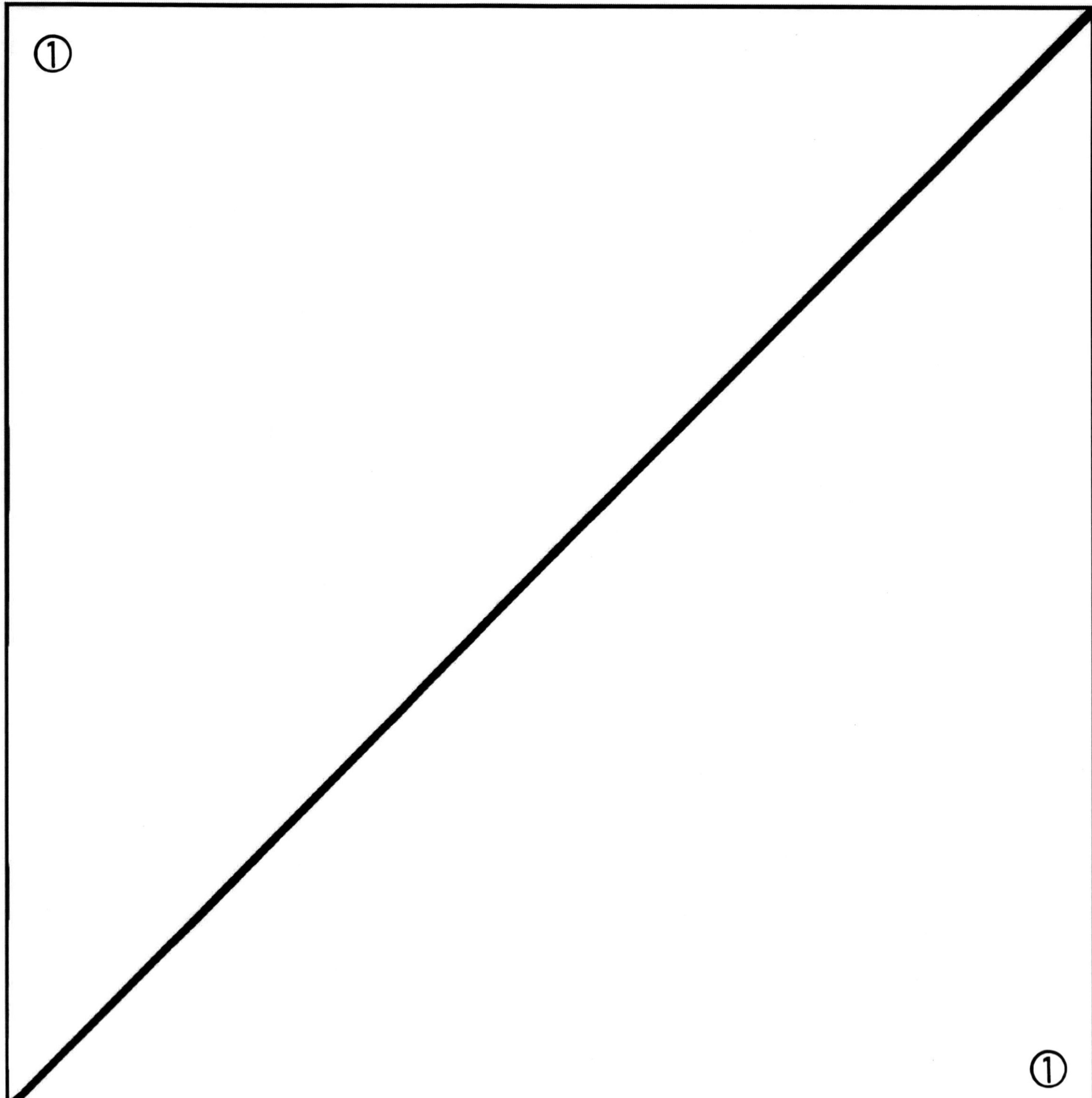
①
①

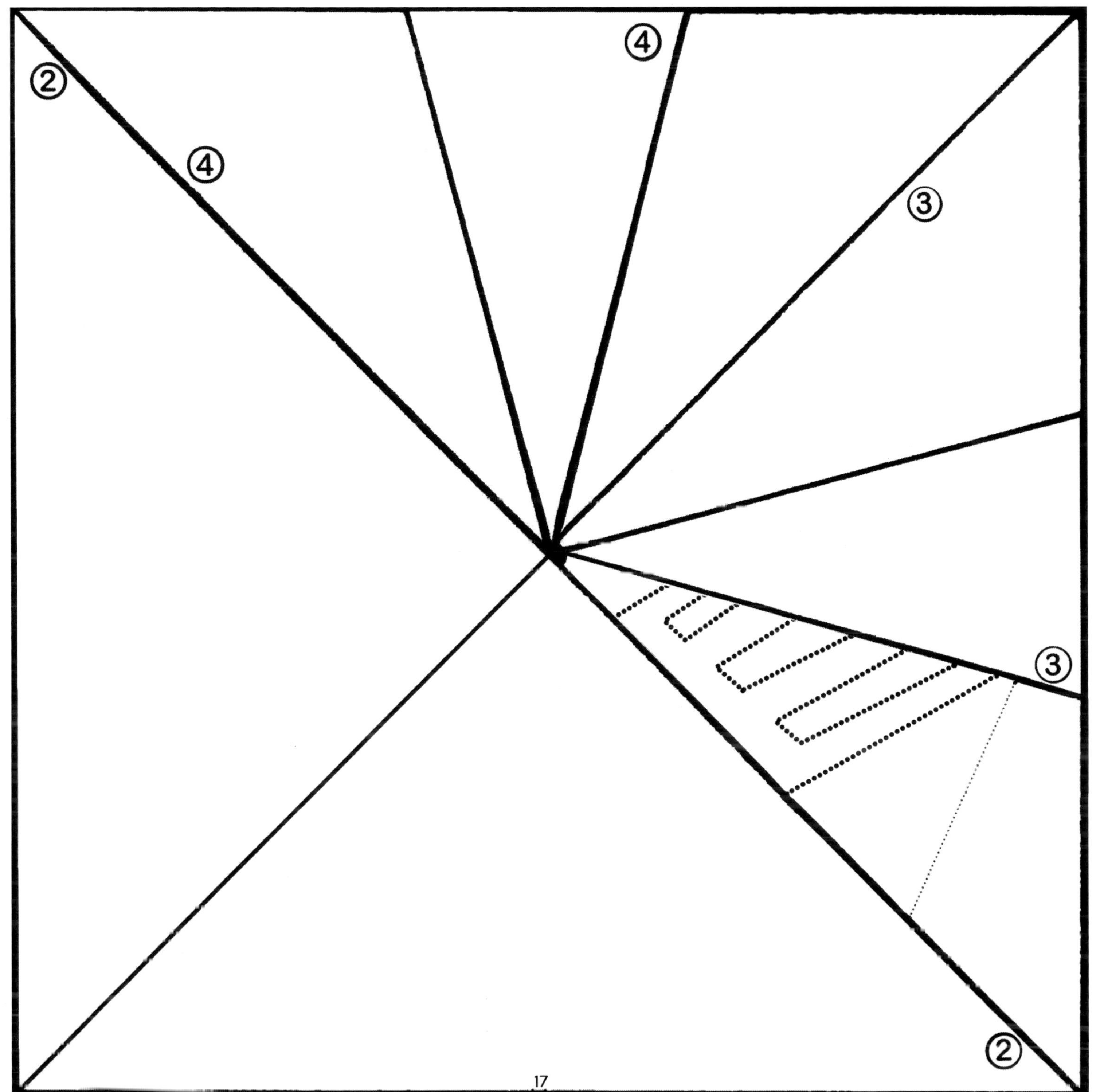
②
④
④
③
③
②

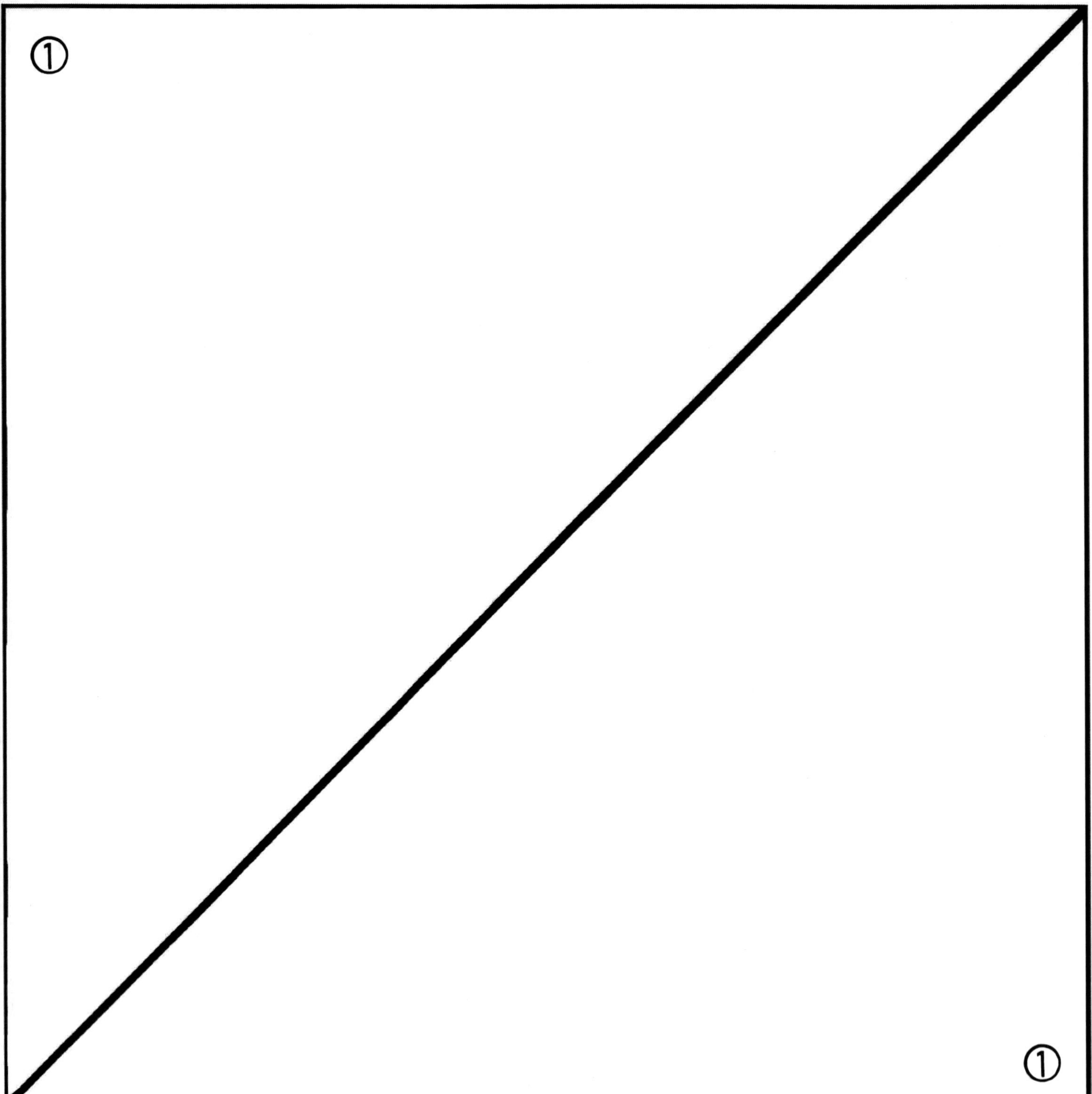
①
①

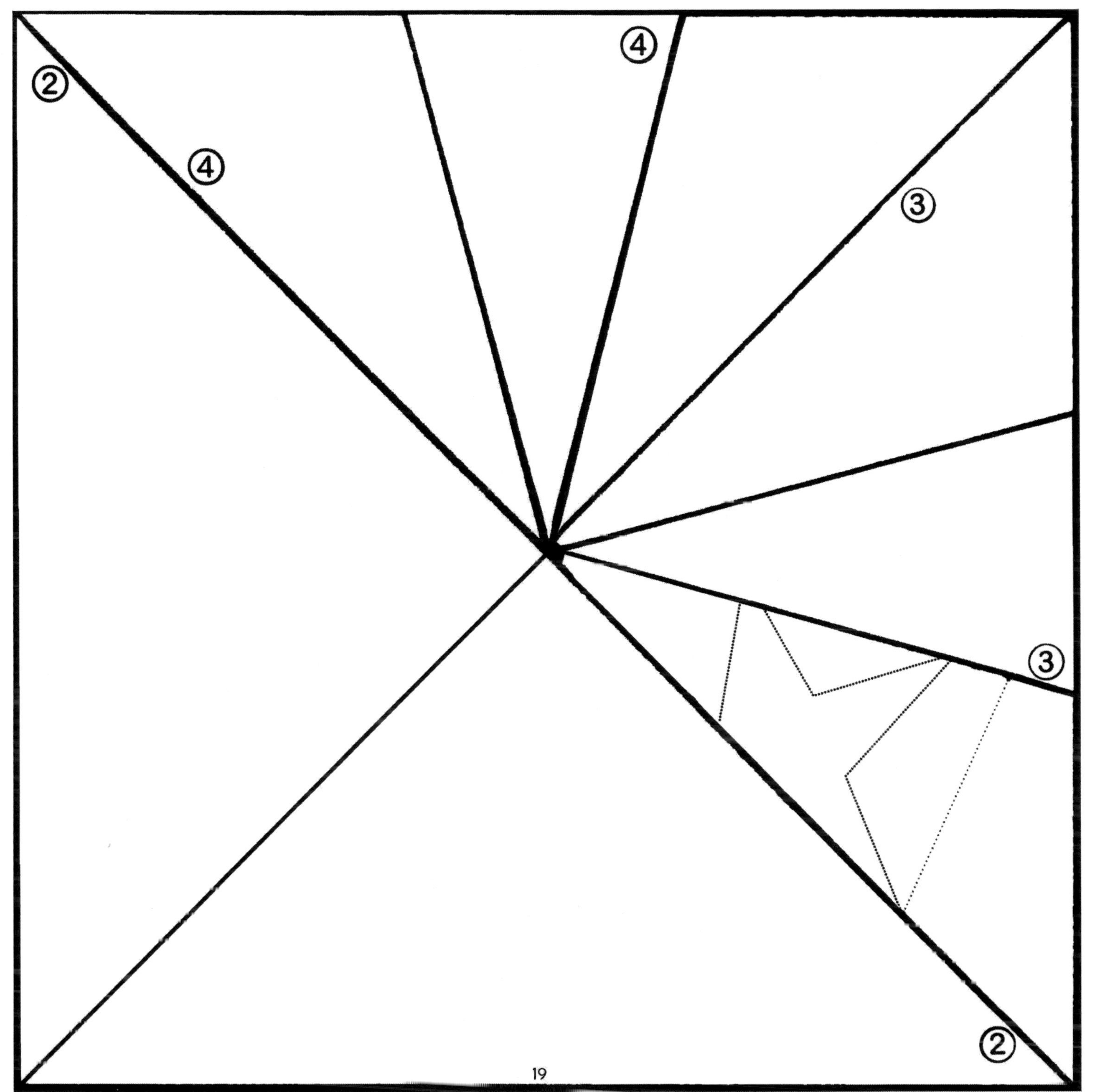
②
④
④
③
③
②

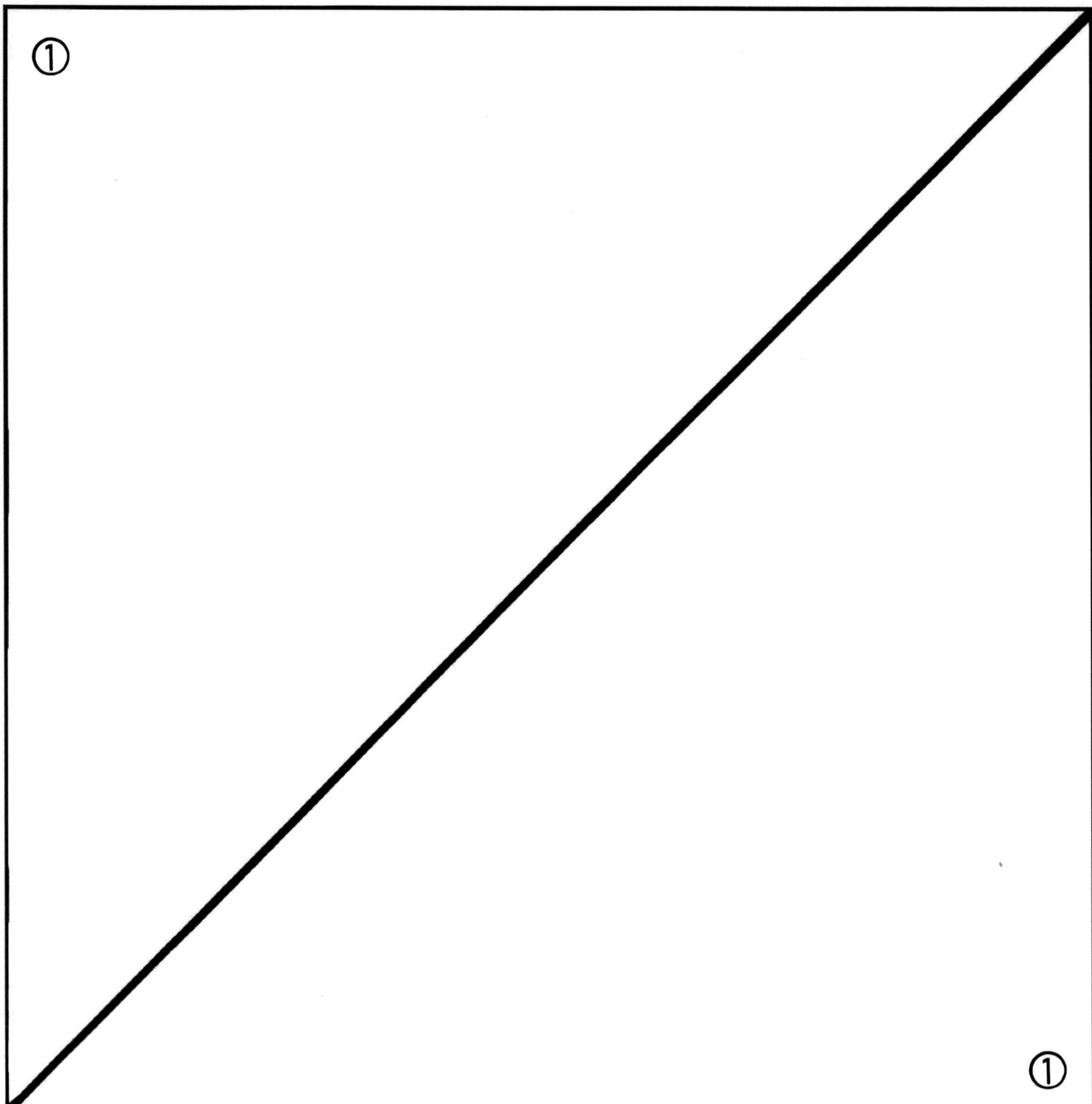
①
①

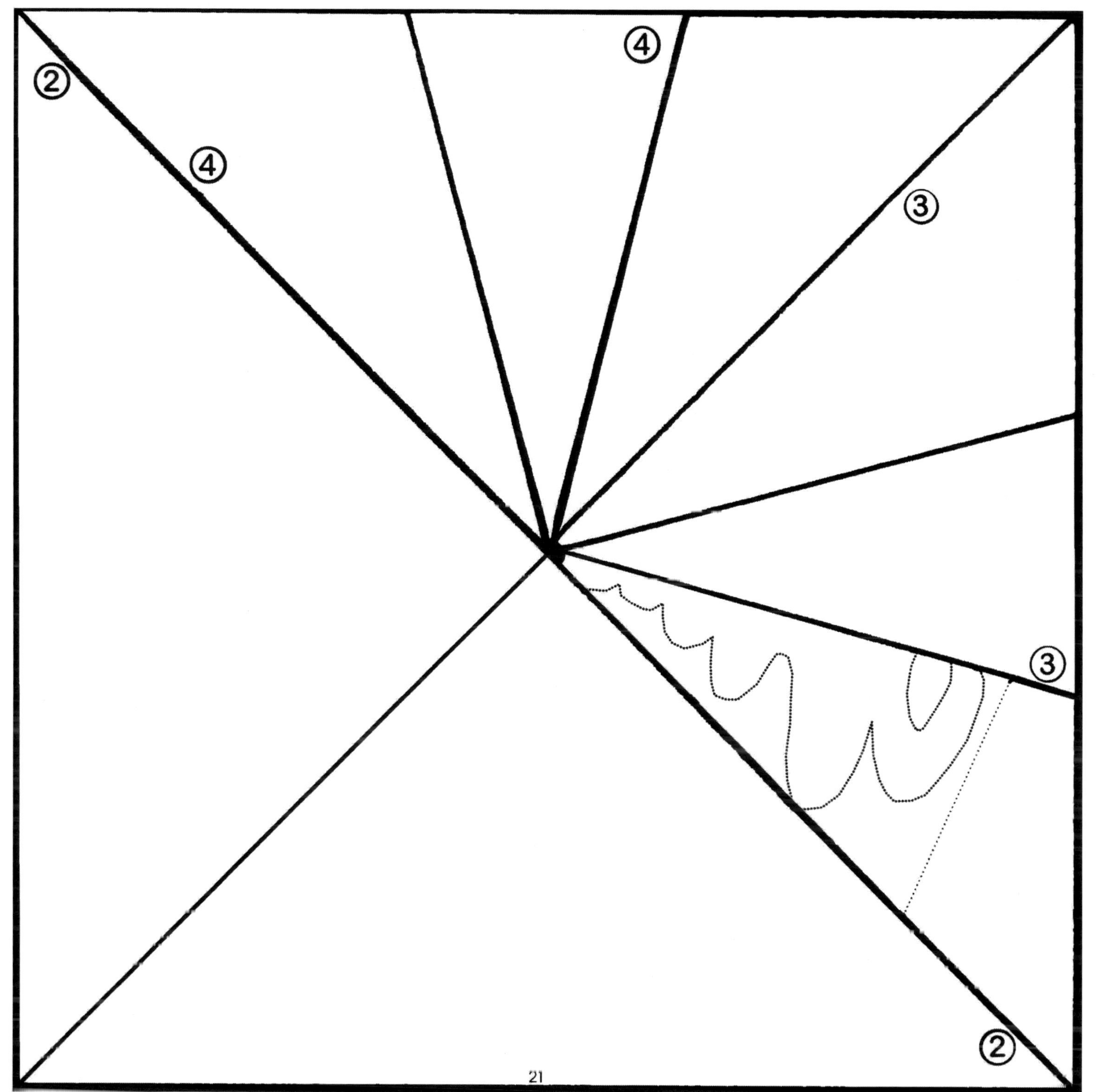
②
④
④
③
③
②

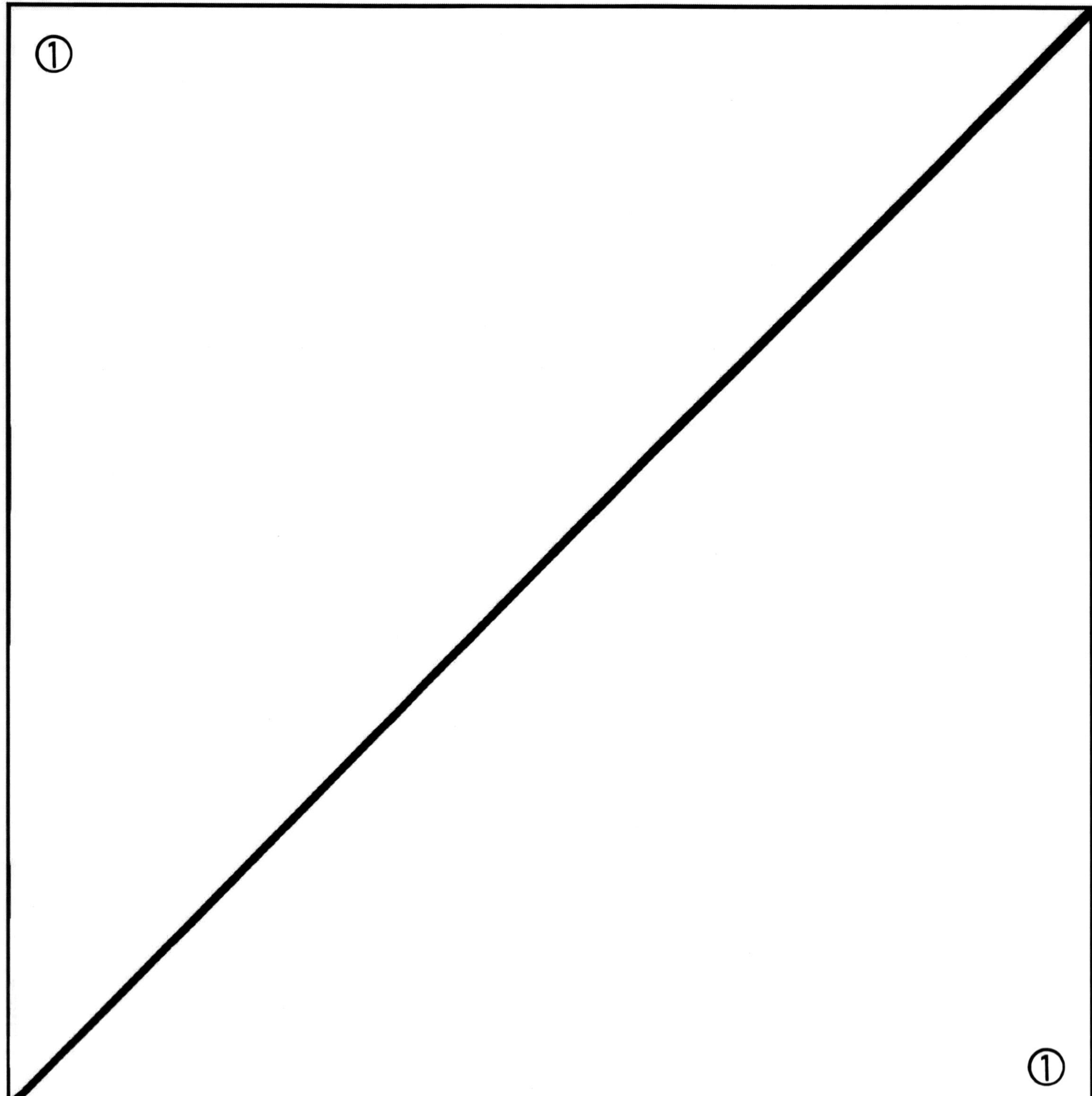
①
①

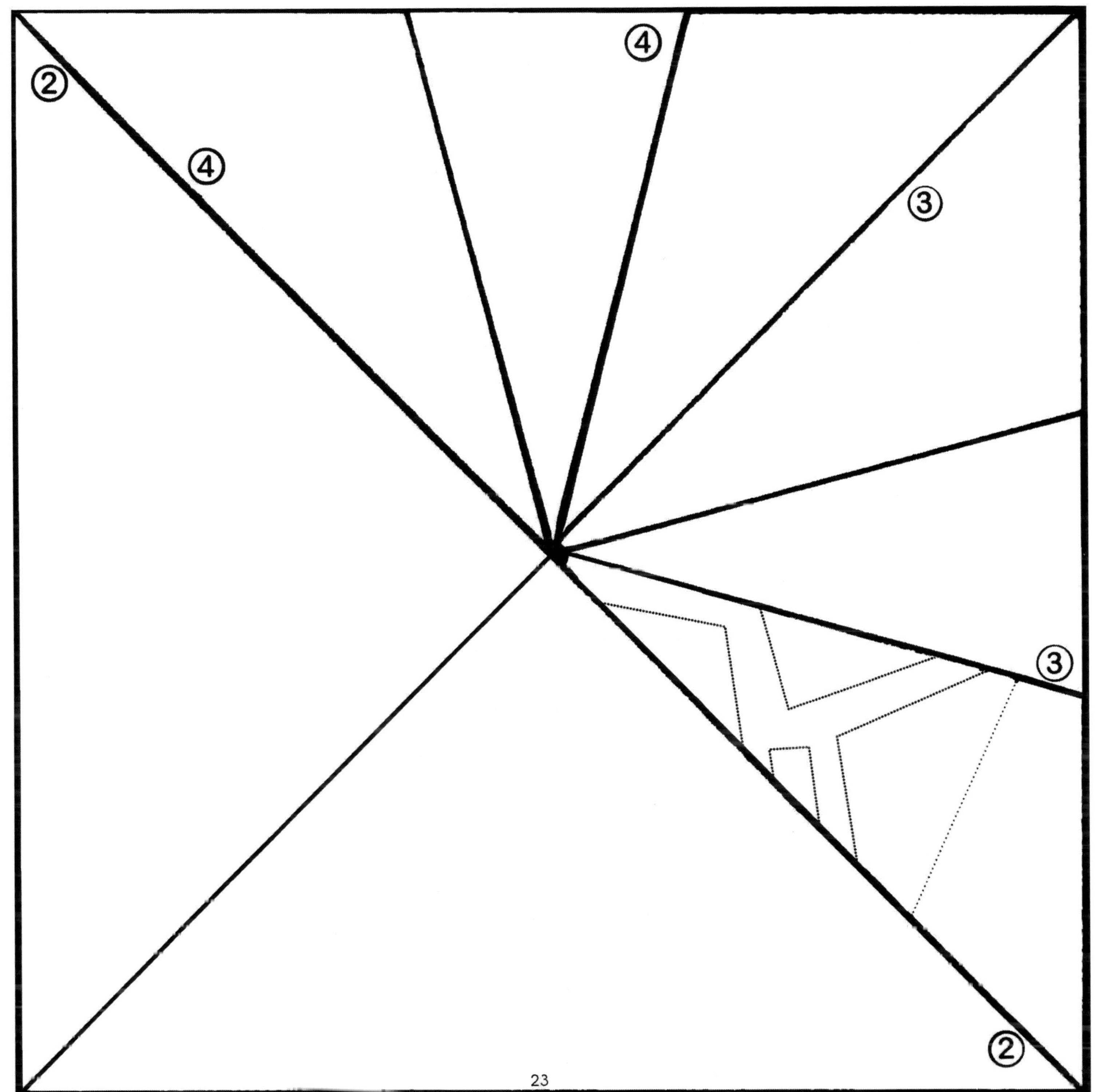
②
④
④
③
③
②

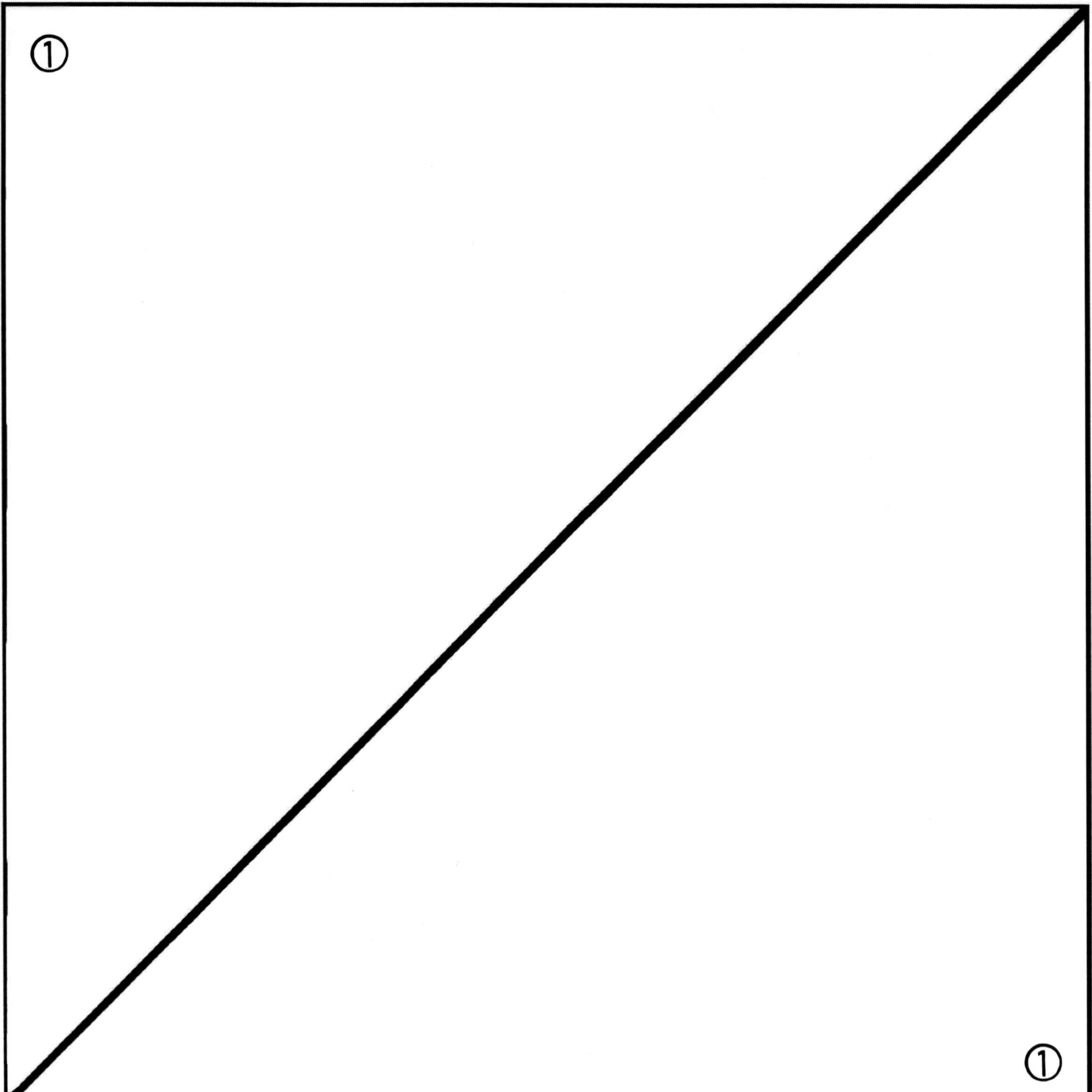
①
①

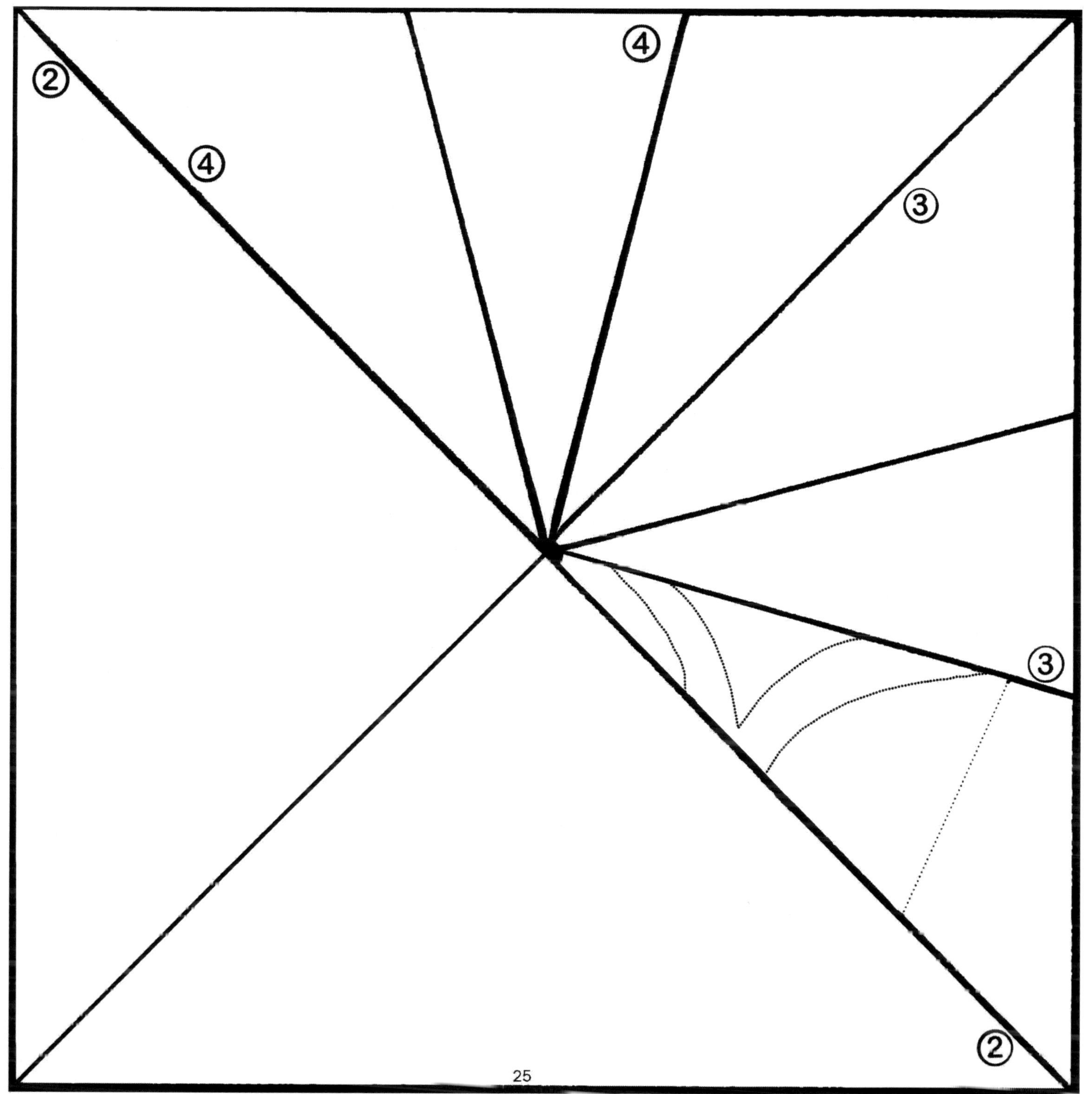
②
④
④
③
③
②

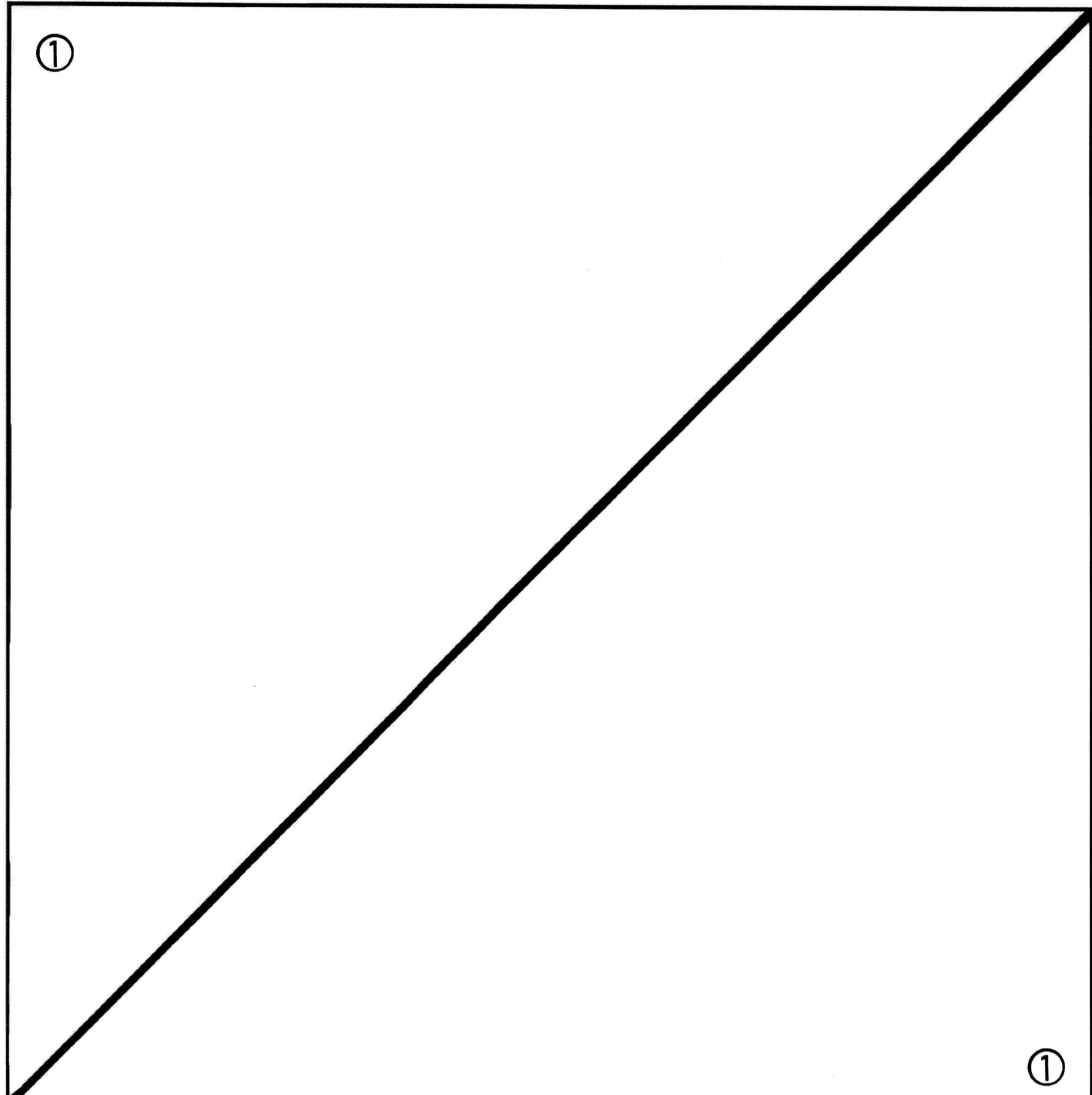

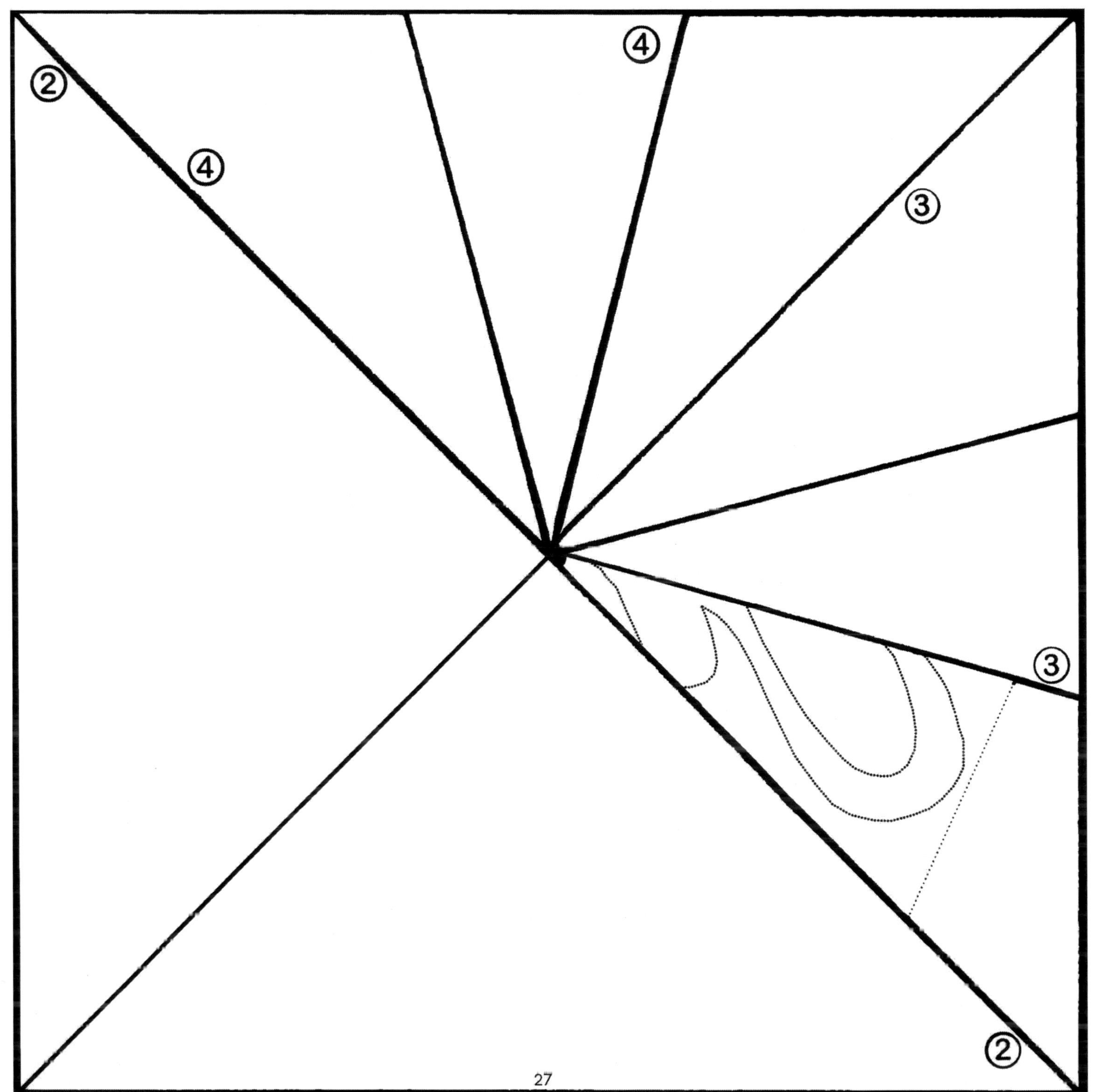
②
④
④
③
③
②

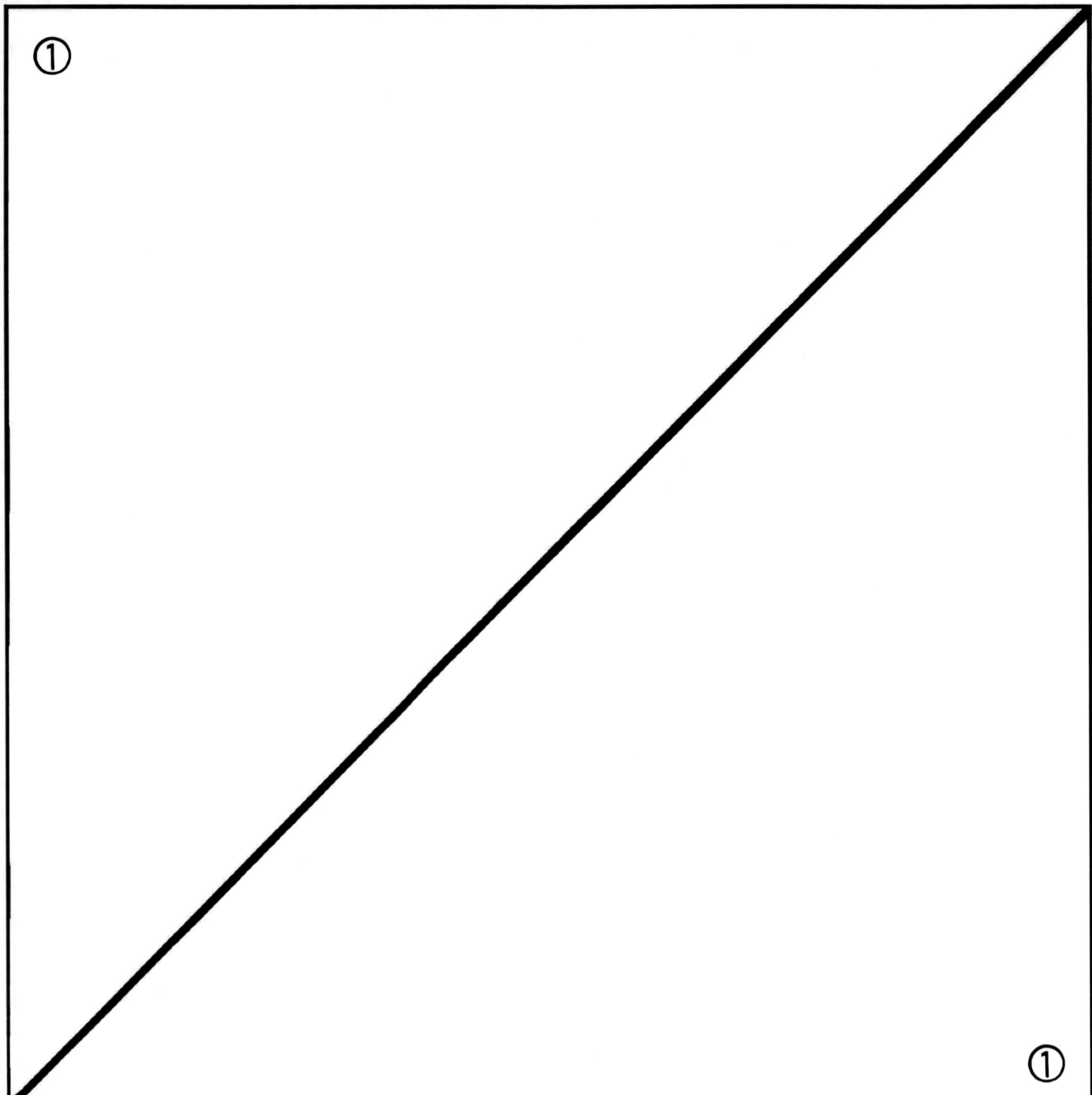
①
①

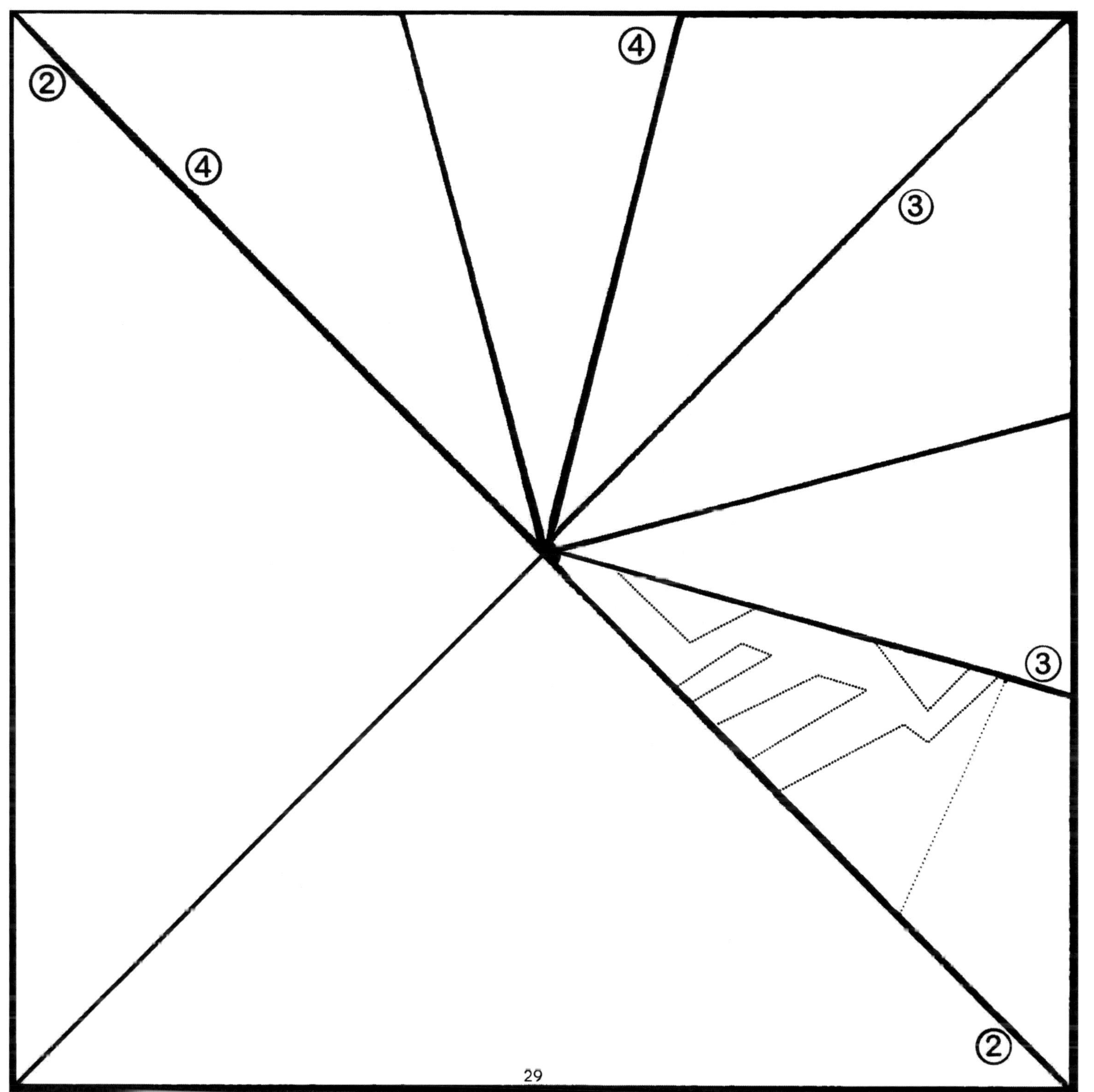
②
④
④
③
③
②

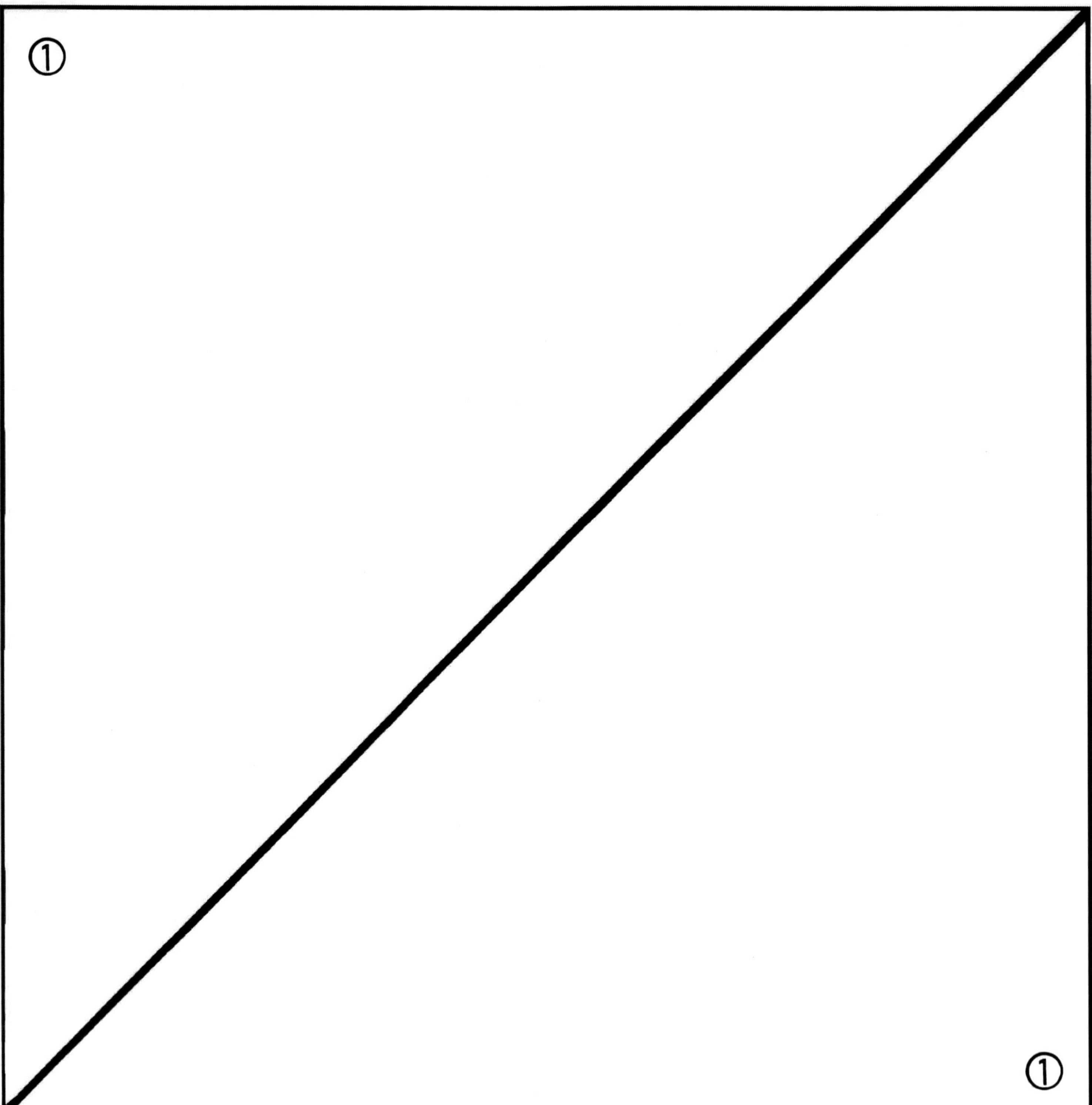
①
①

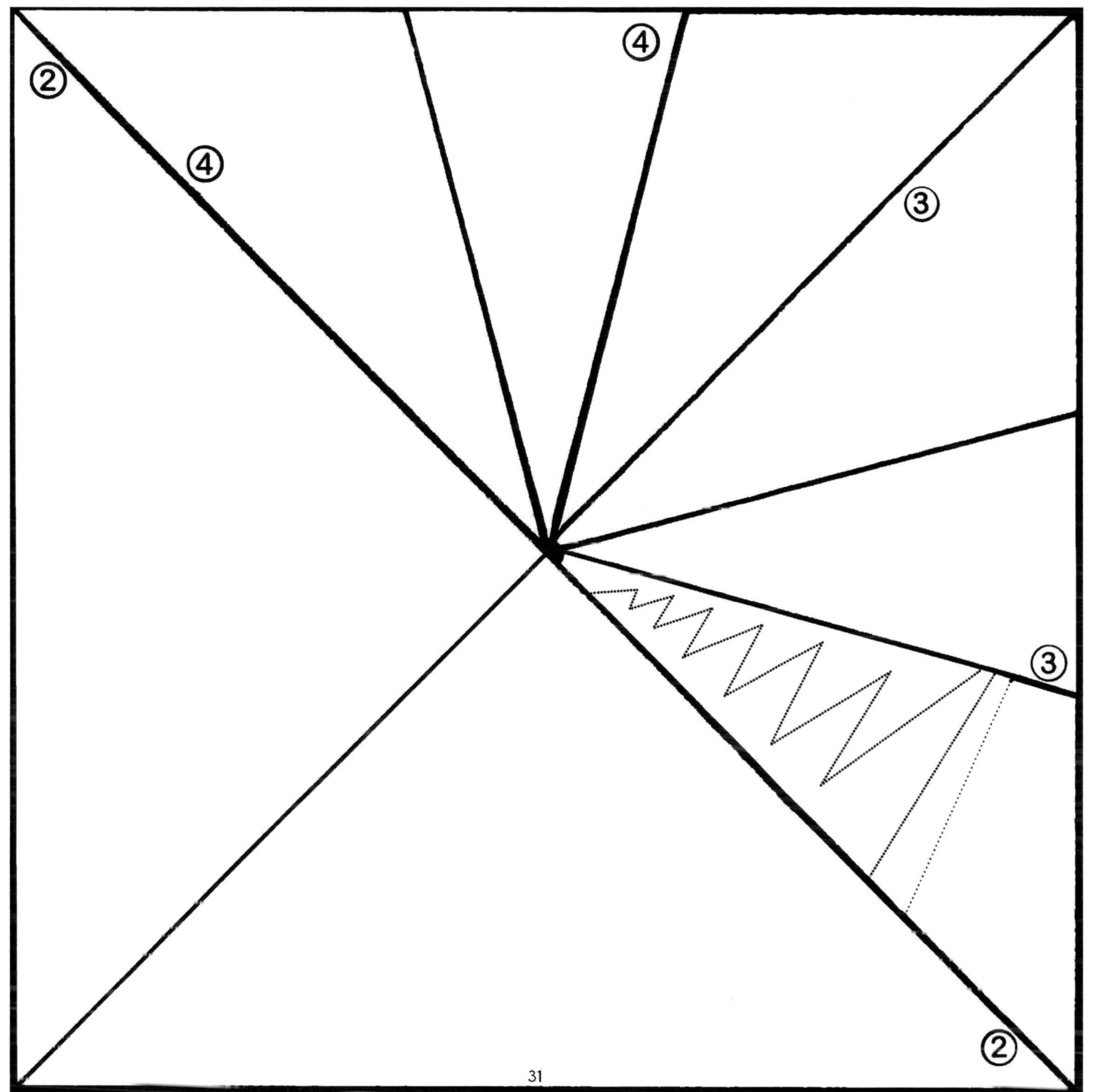
②
④
④
③
③
②

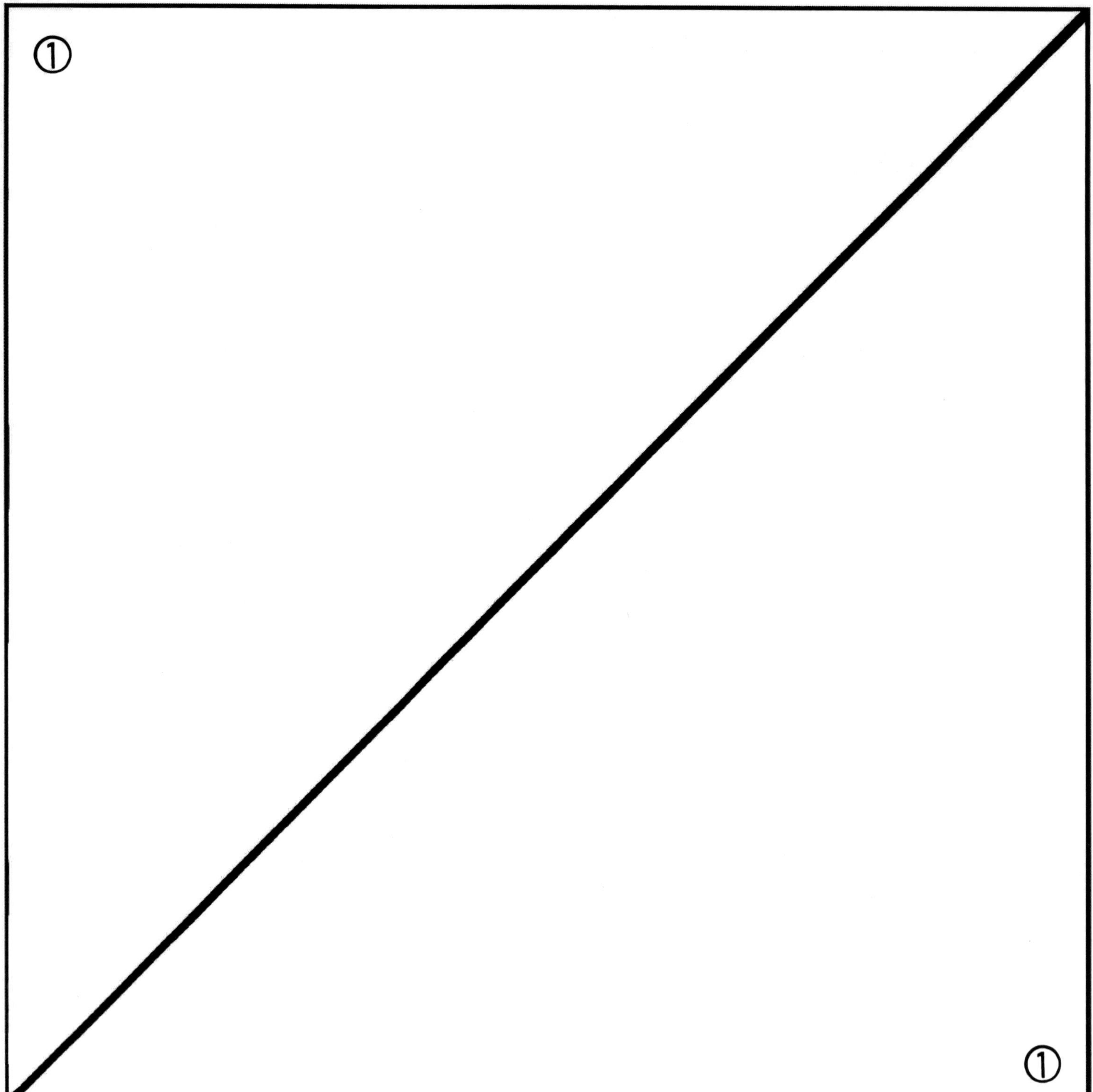
①
①

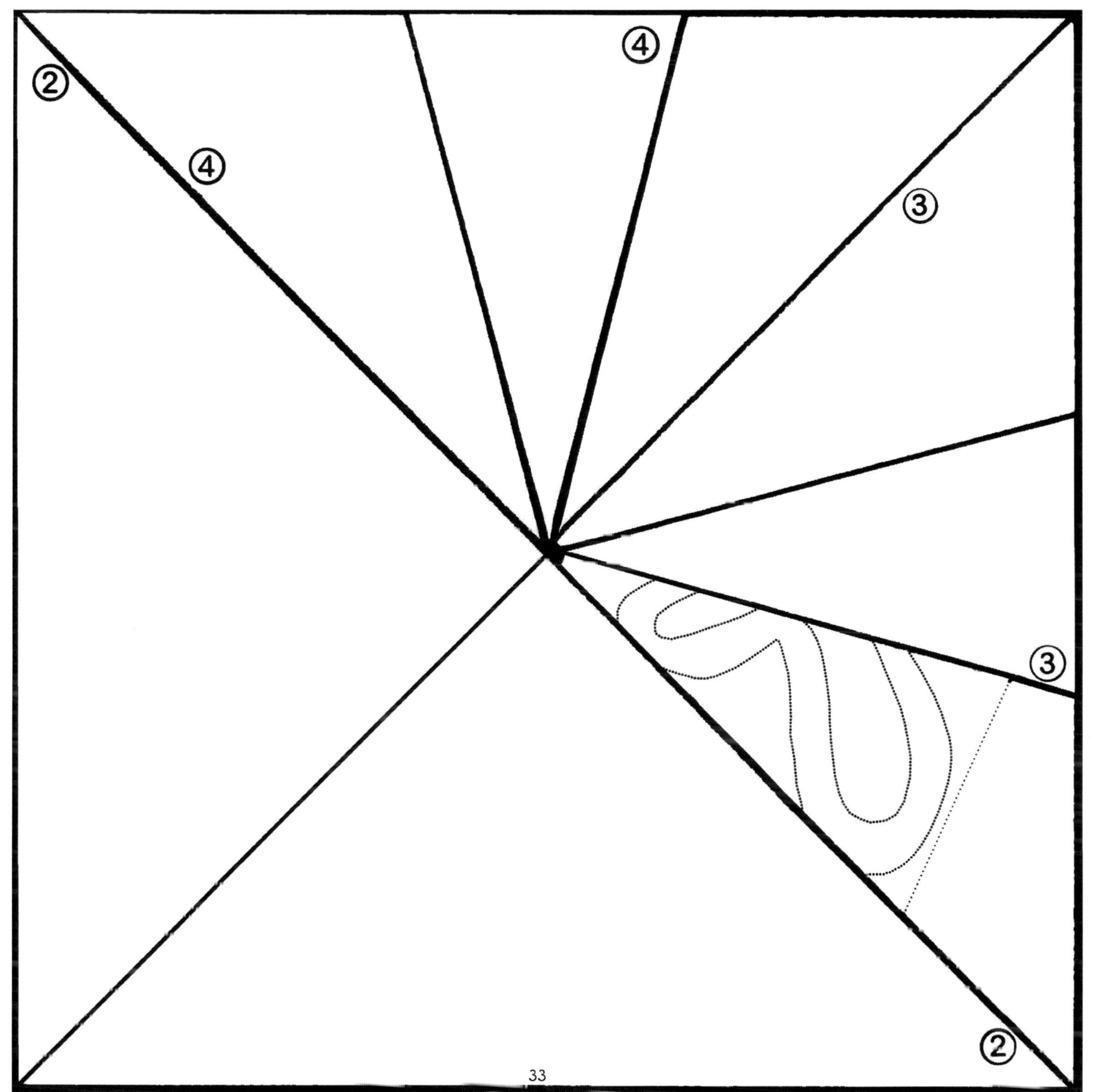
②
④
④
③
③
②

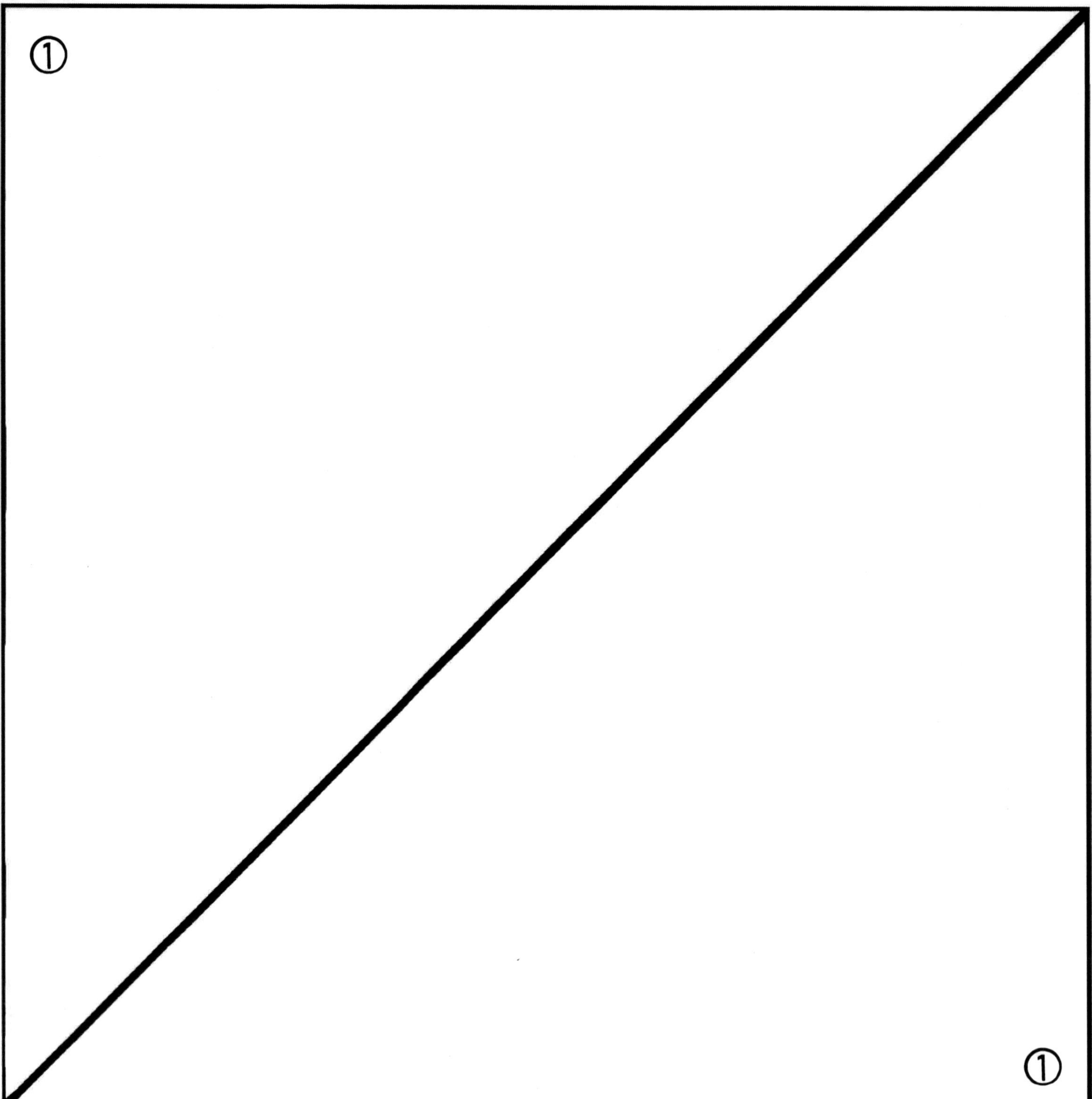
①
①

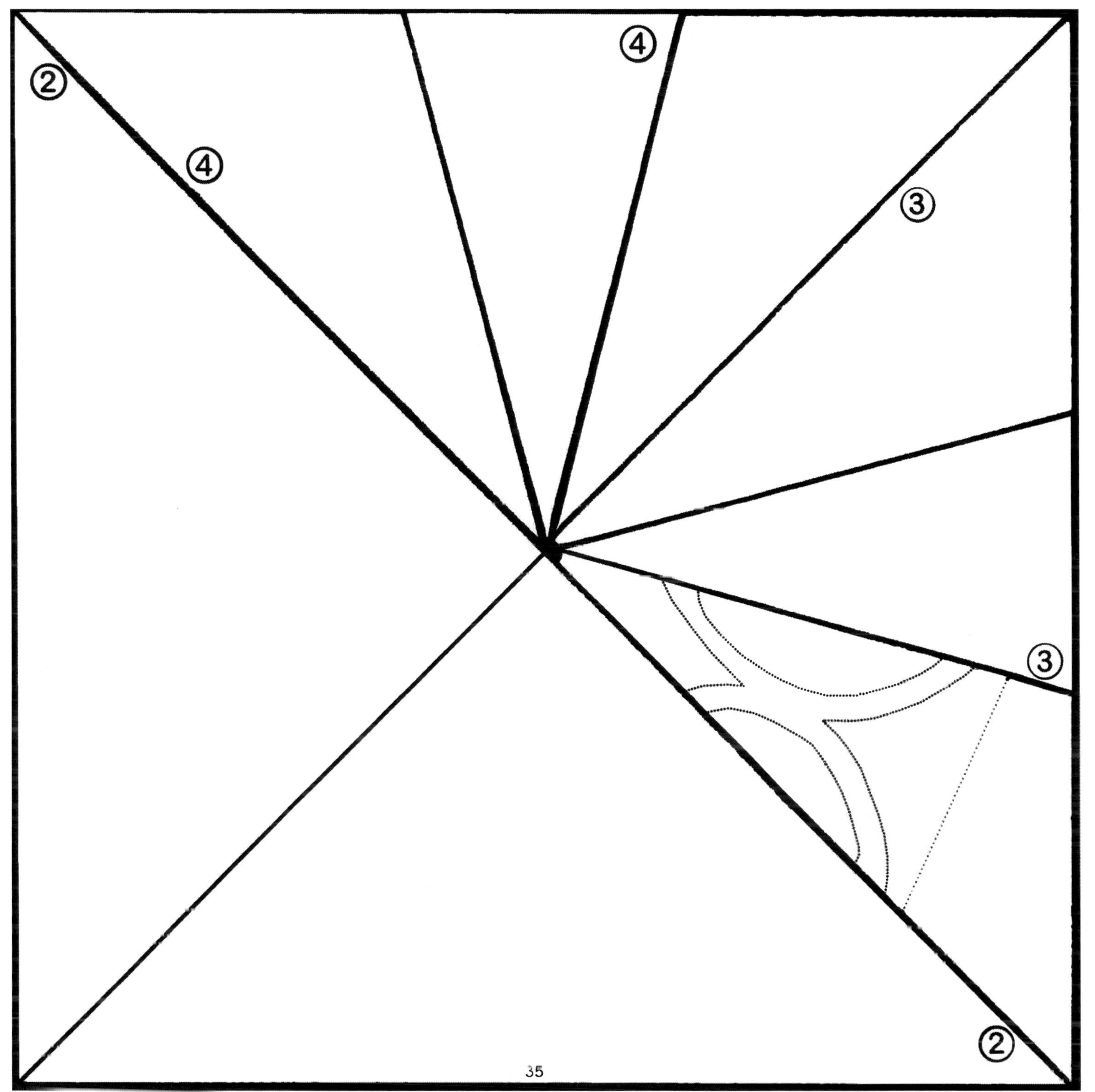
②
④
④
③
③
②

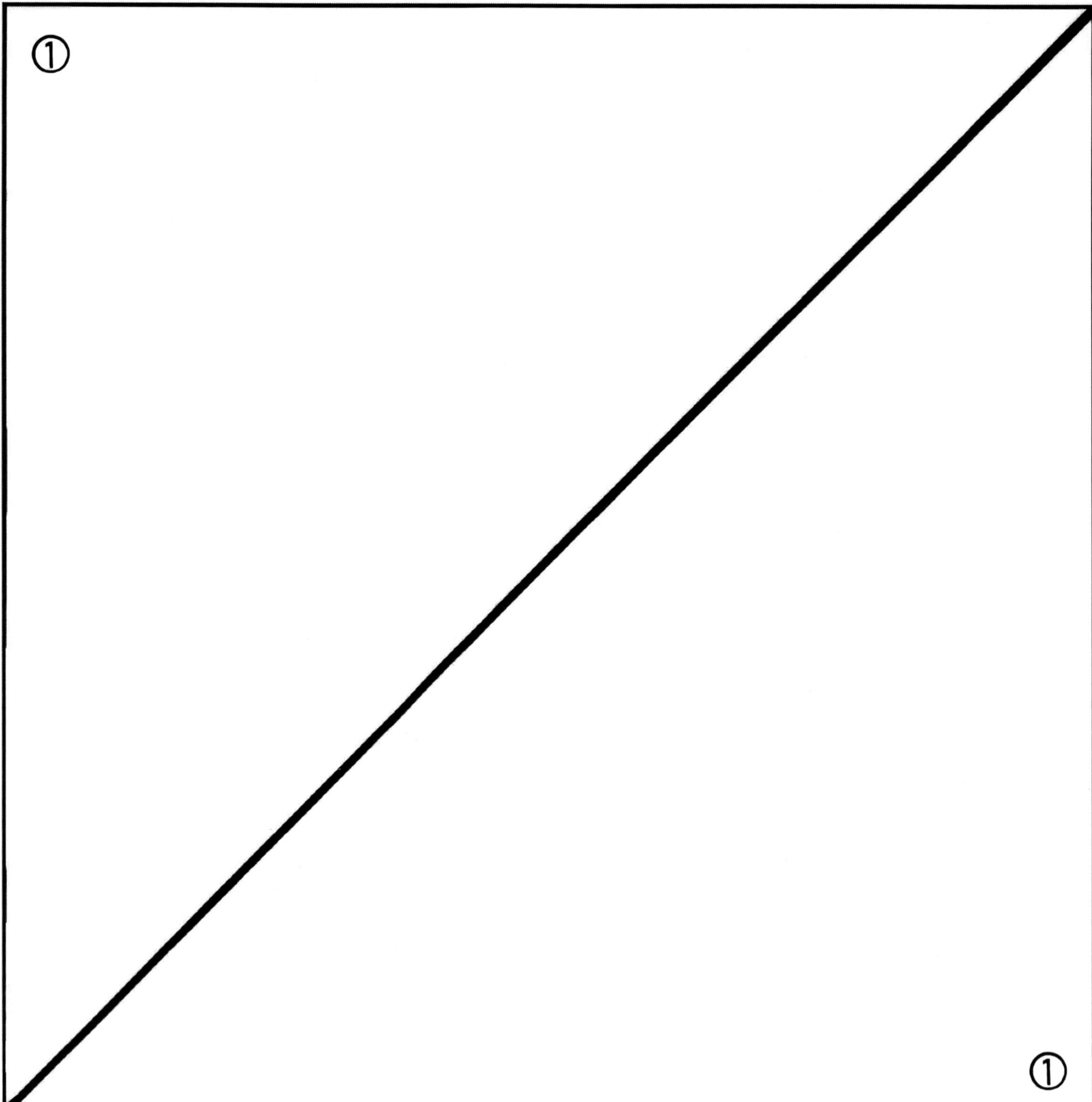
①
①

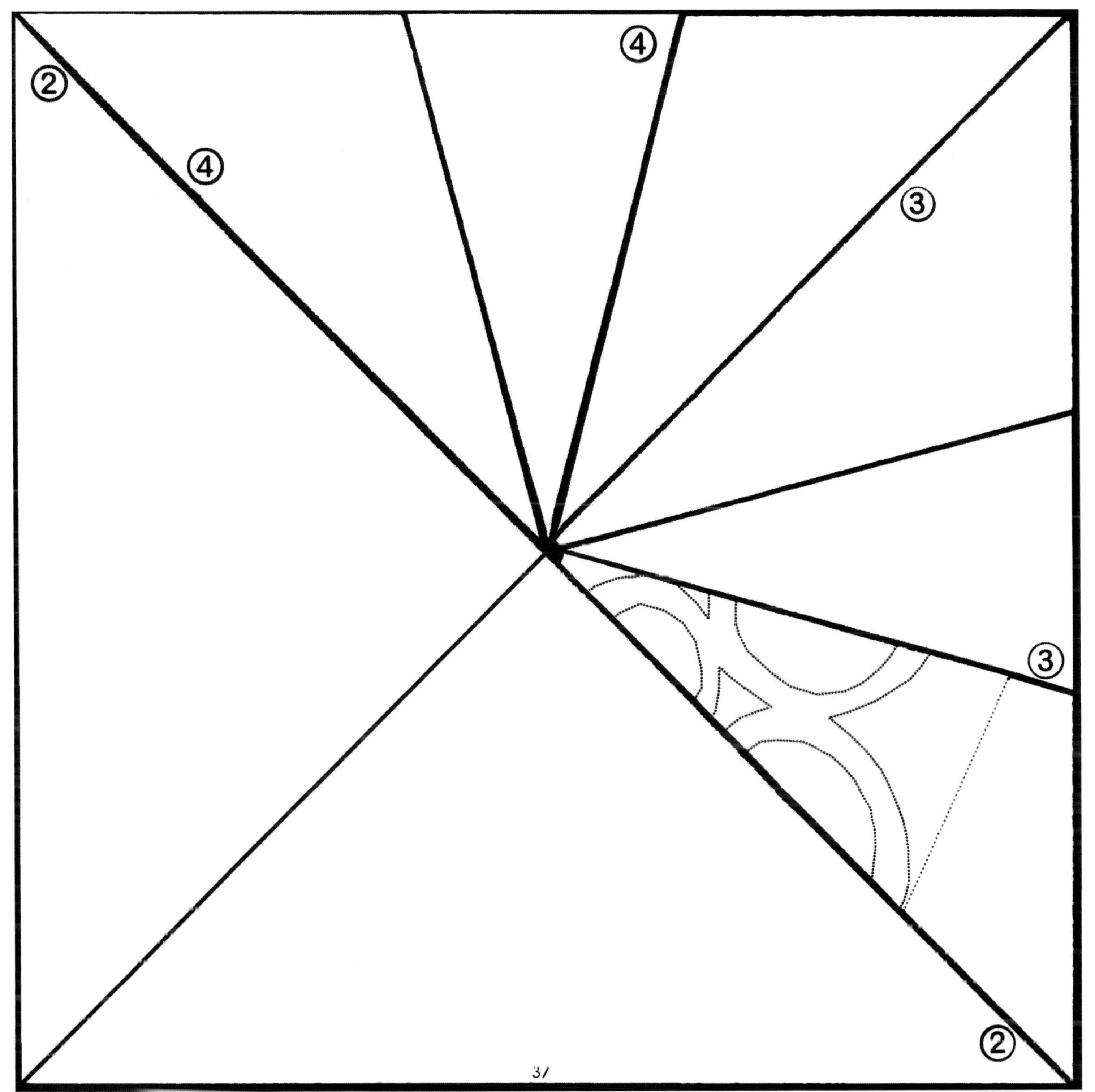
②
④
④
③
③
②

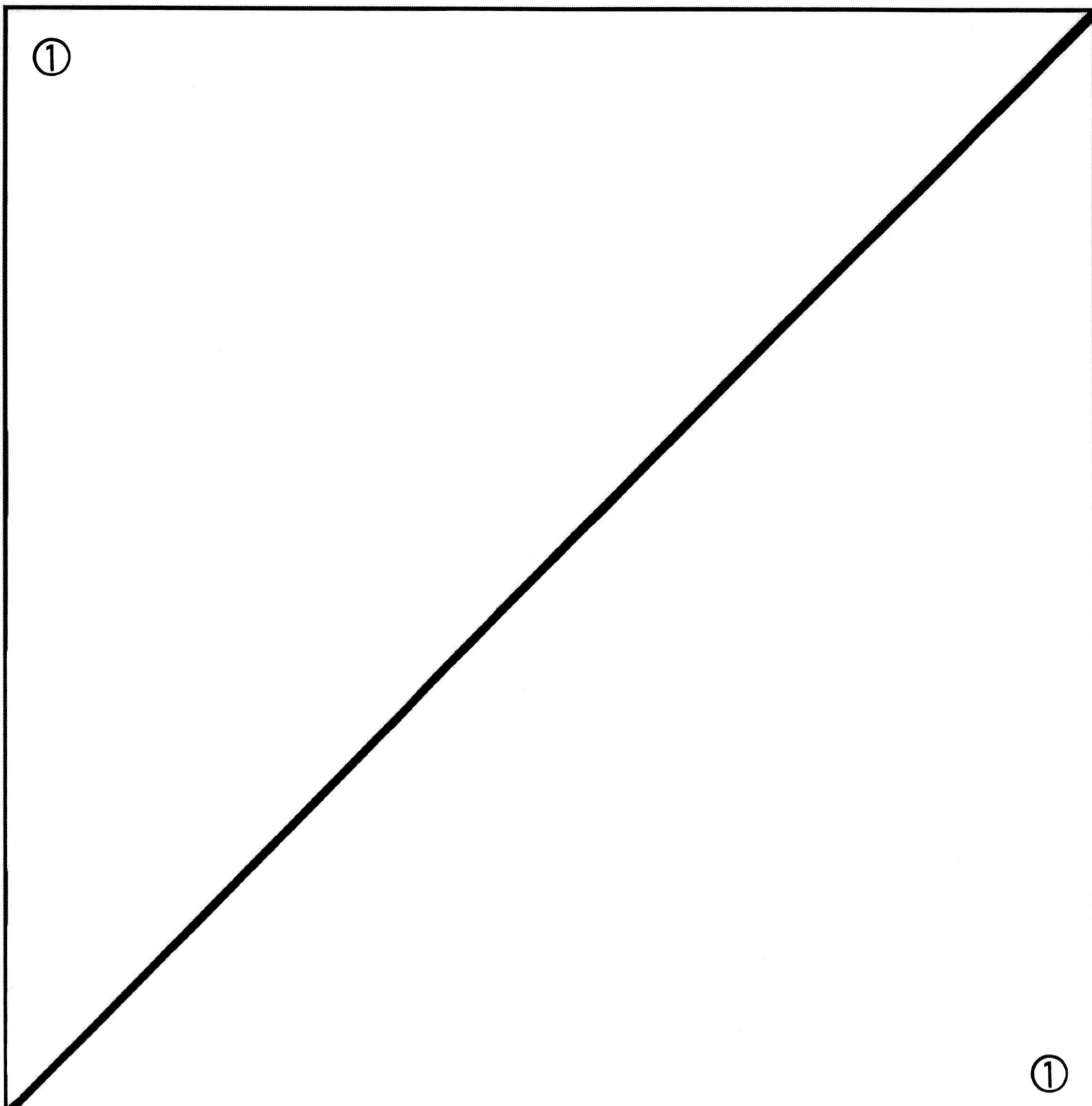
①
①

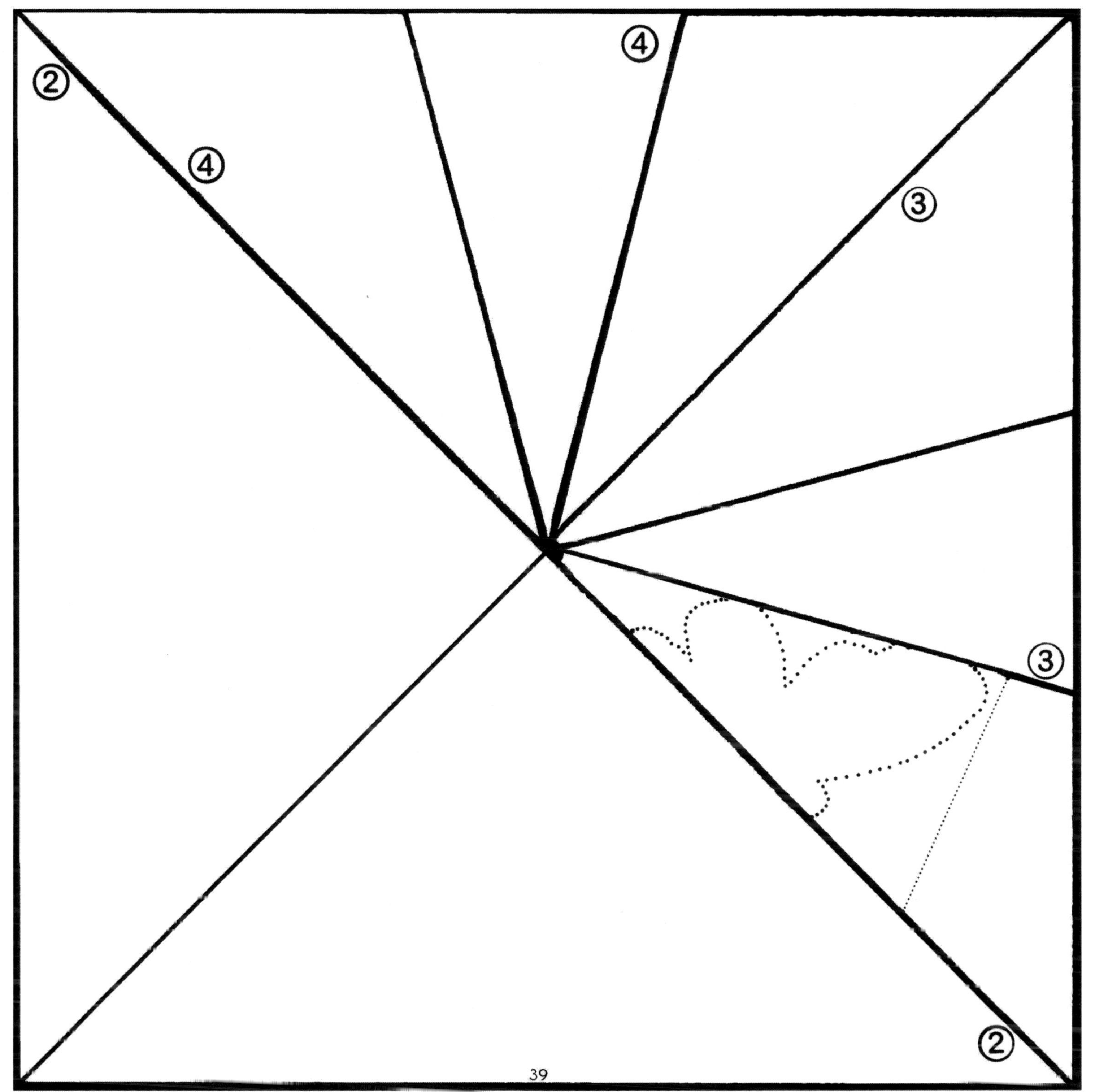
②
④
④
③
③
②

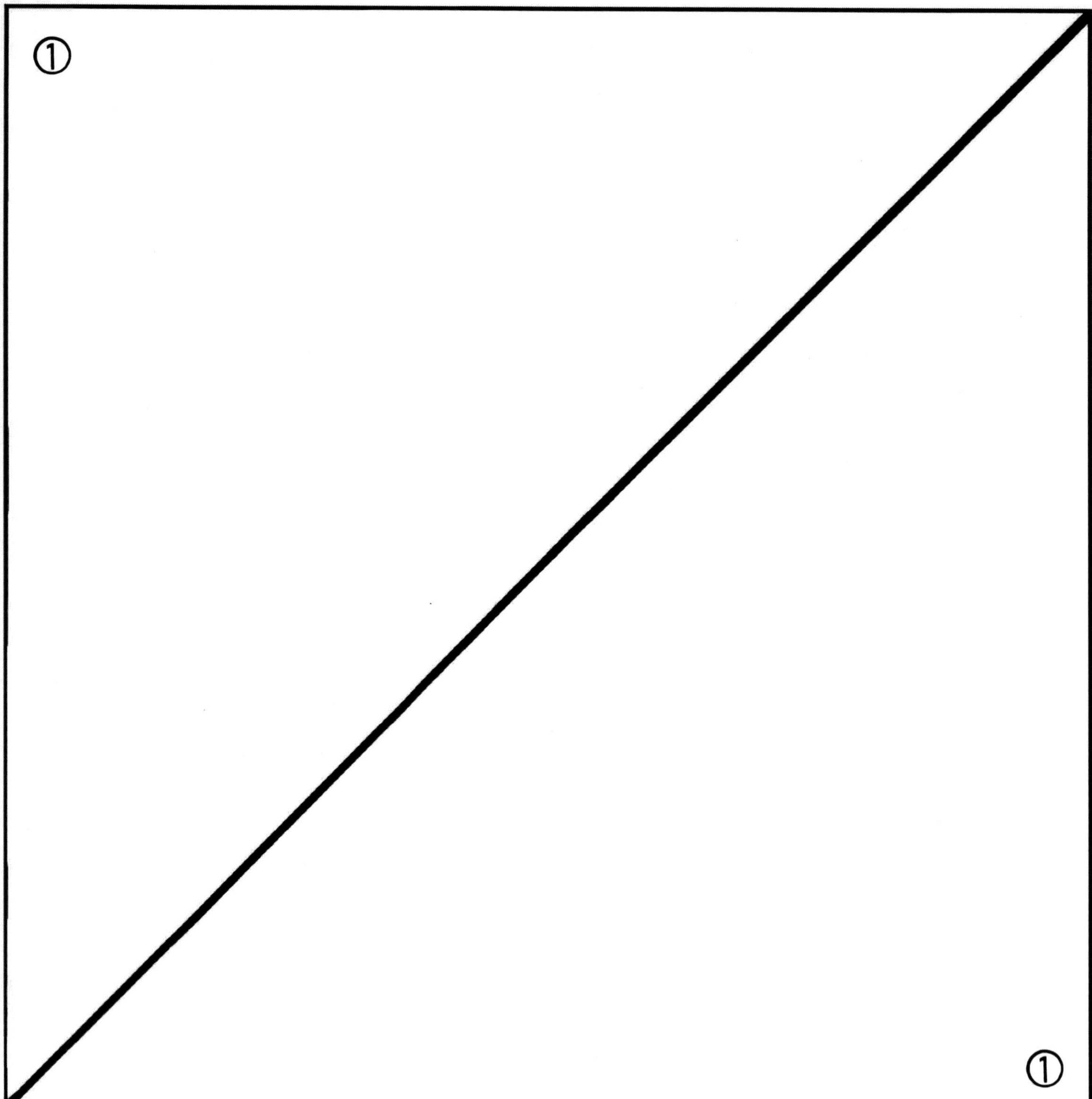
①
①

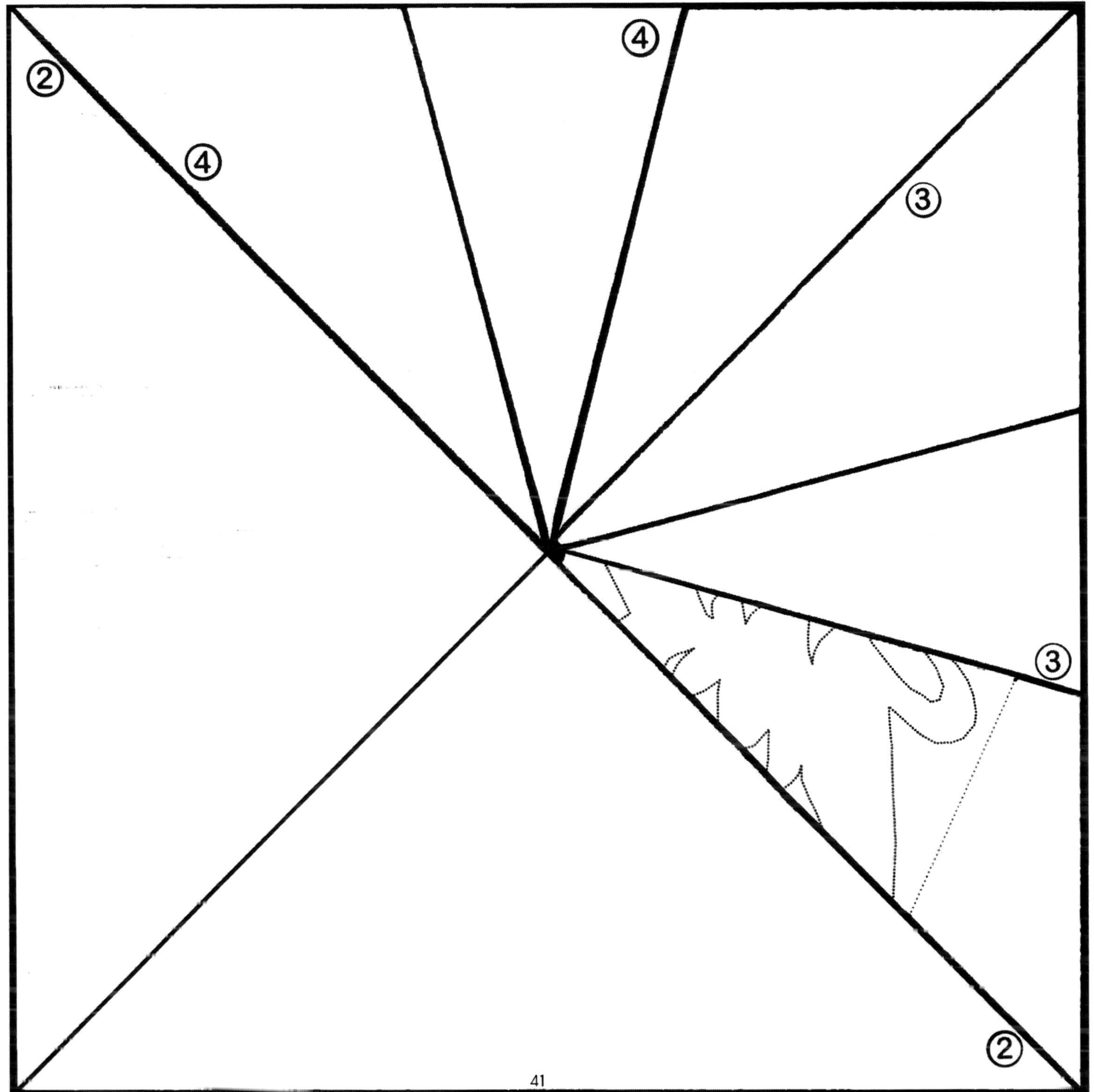
②
④
④
③
③
②

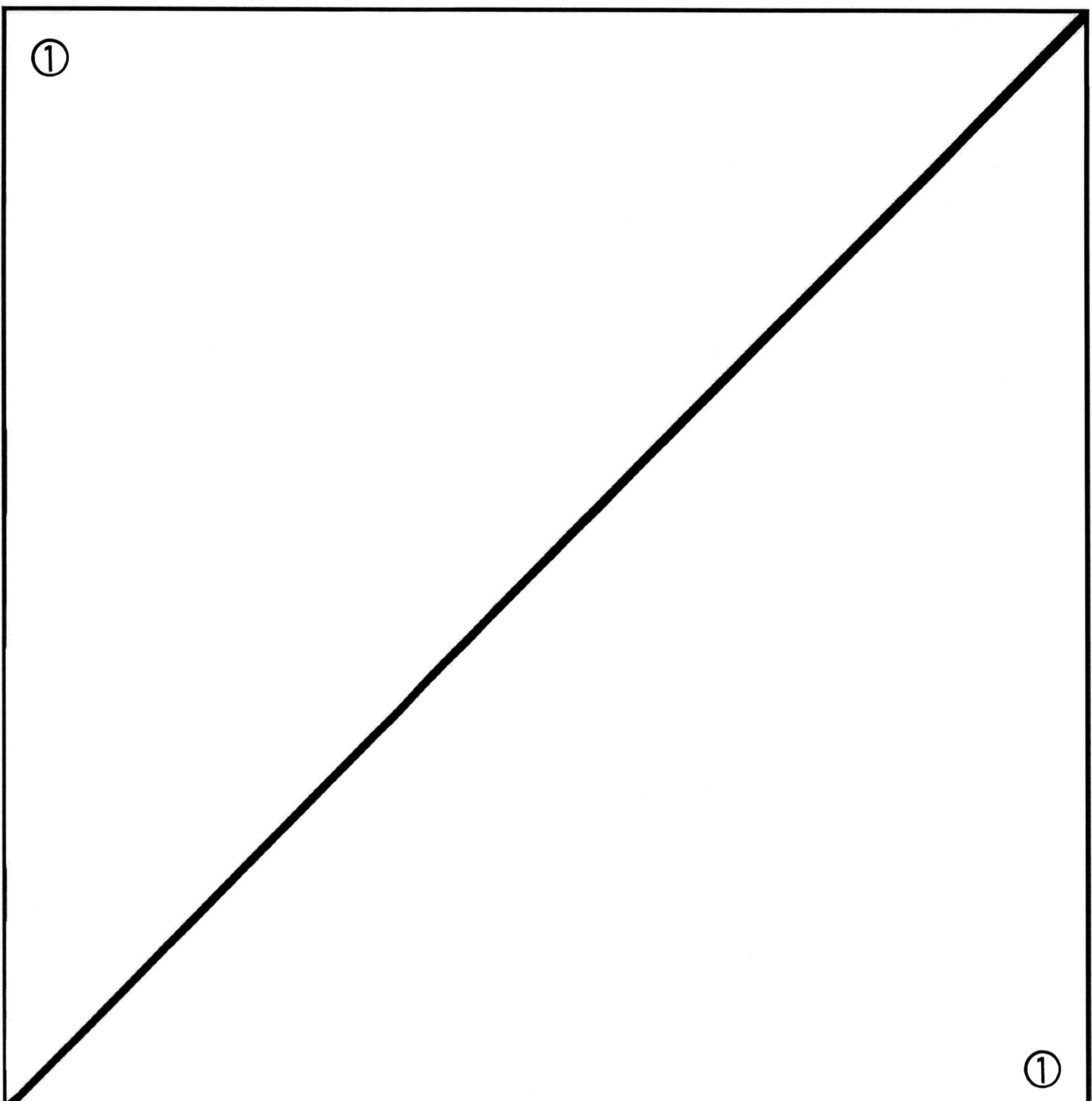
①
①

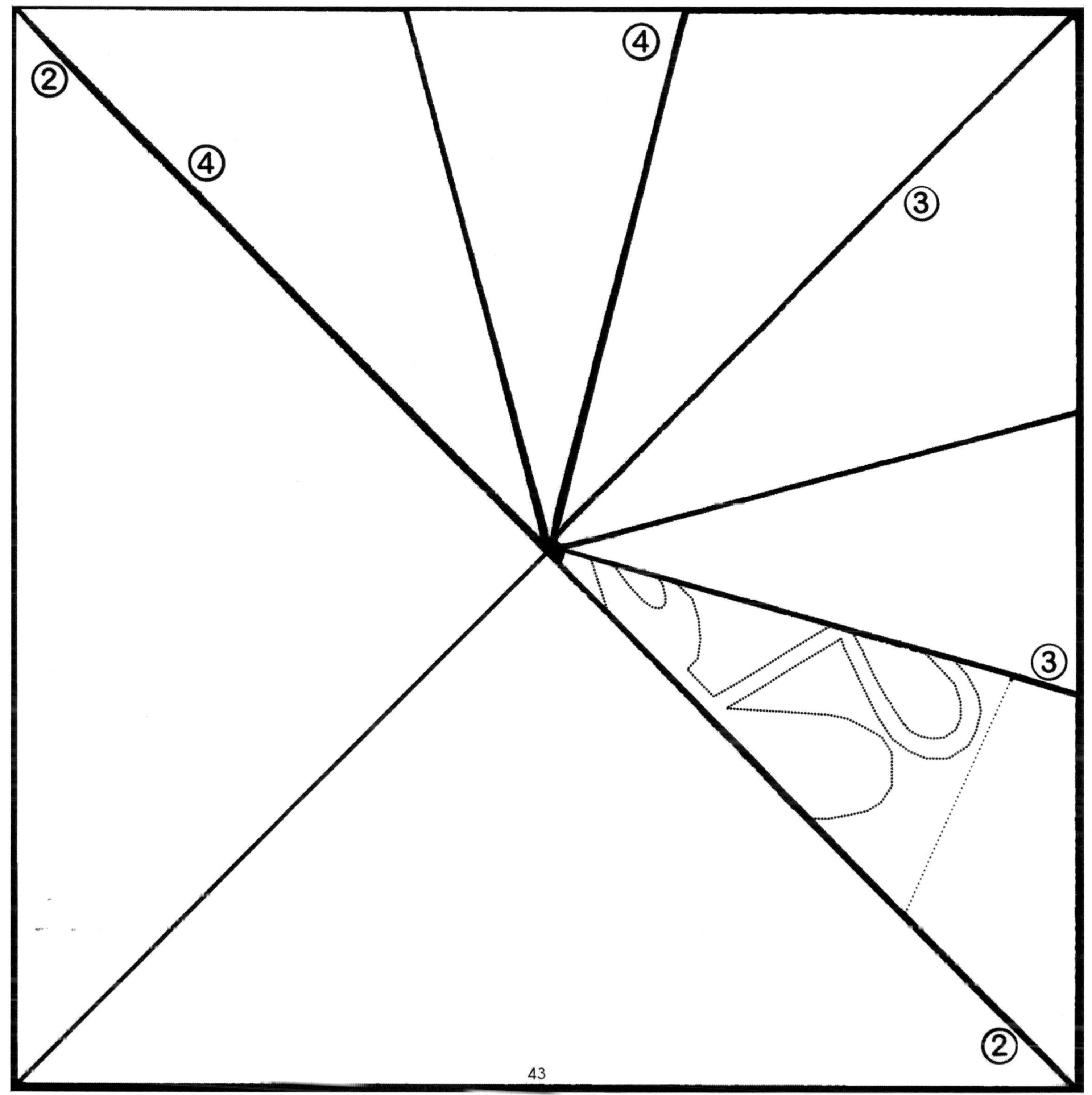
②
④
④
③
③
②

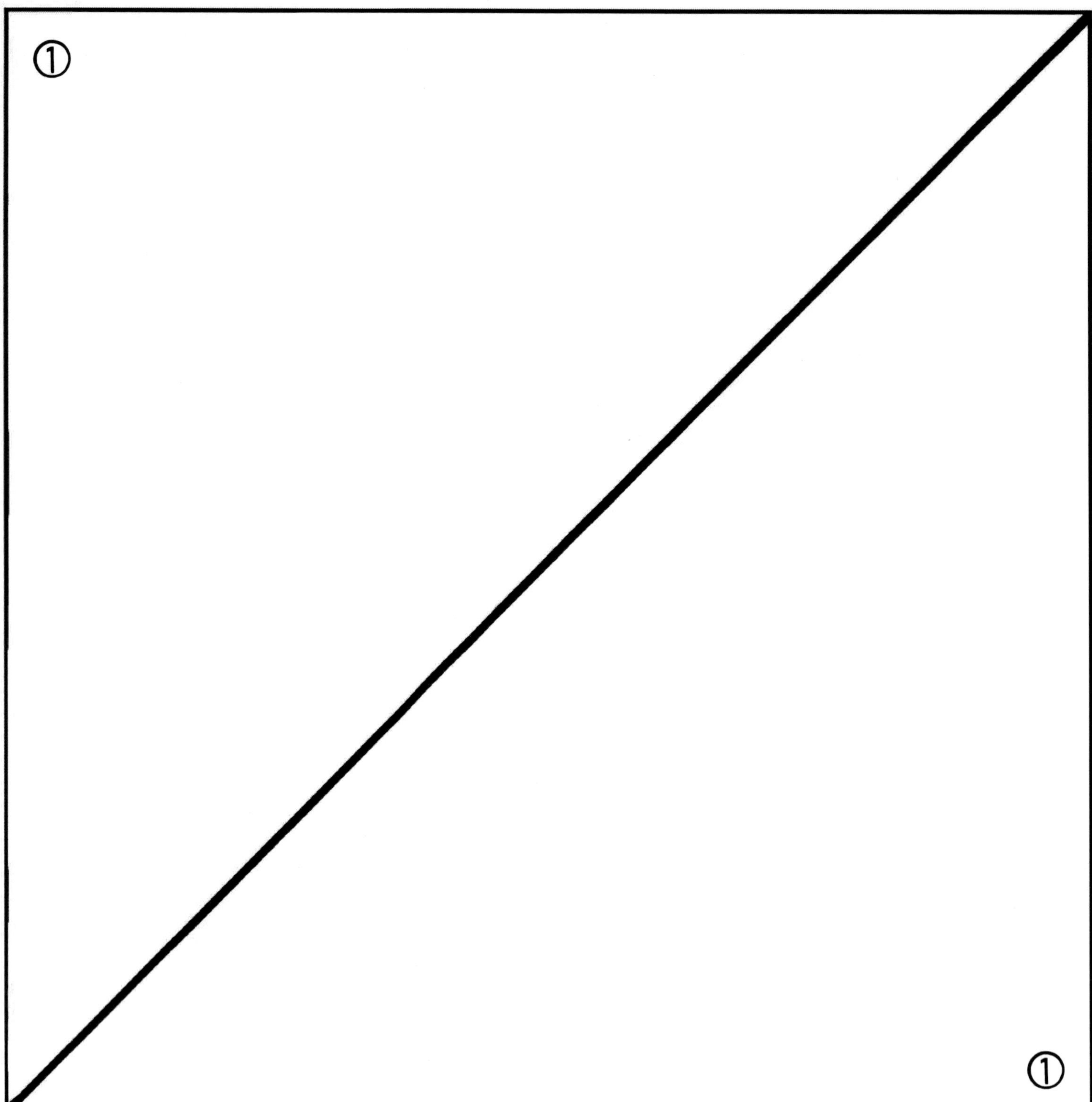
①
①

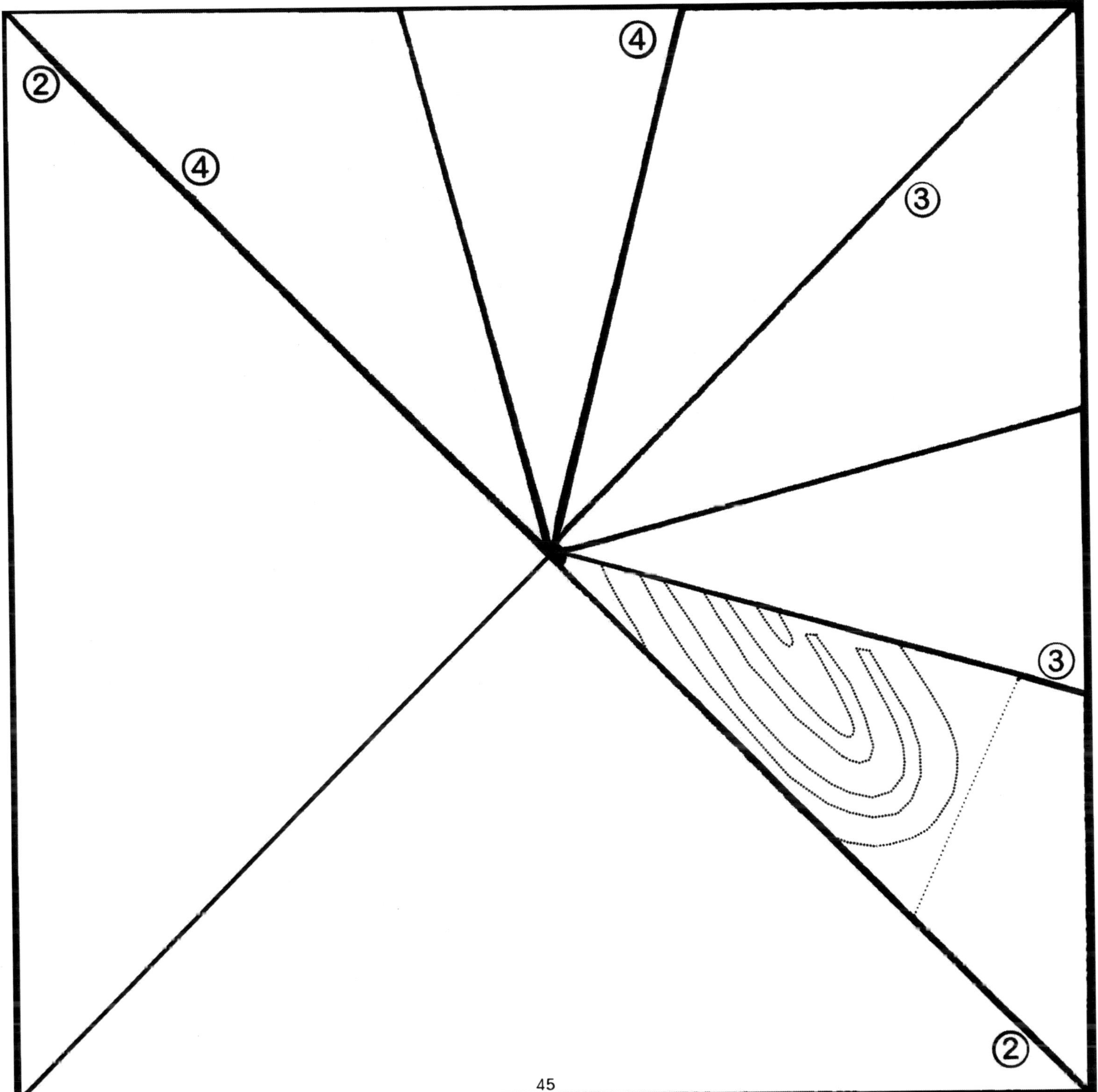
②
④
④
③
③
②

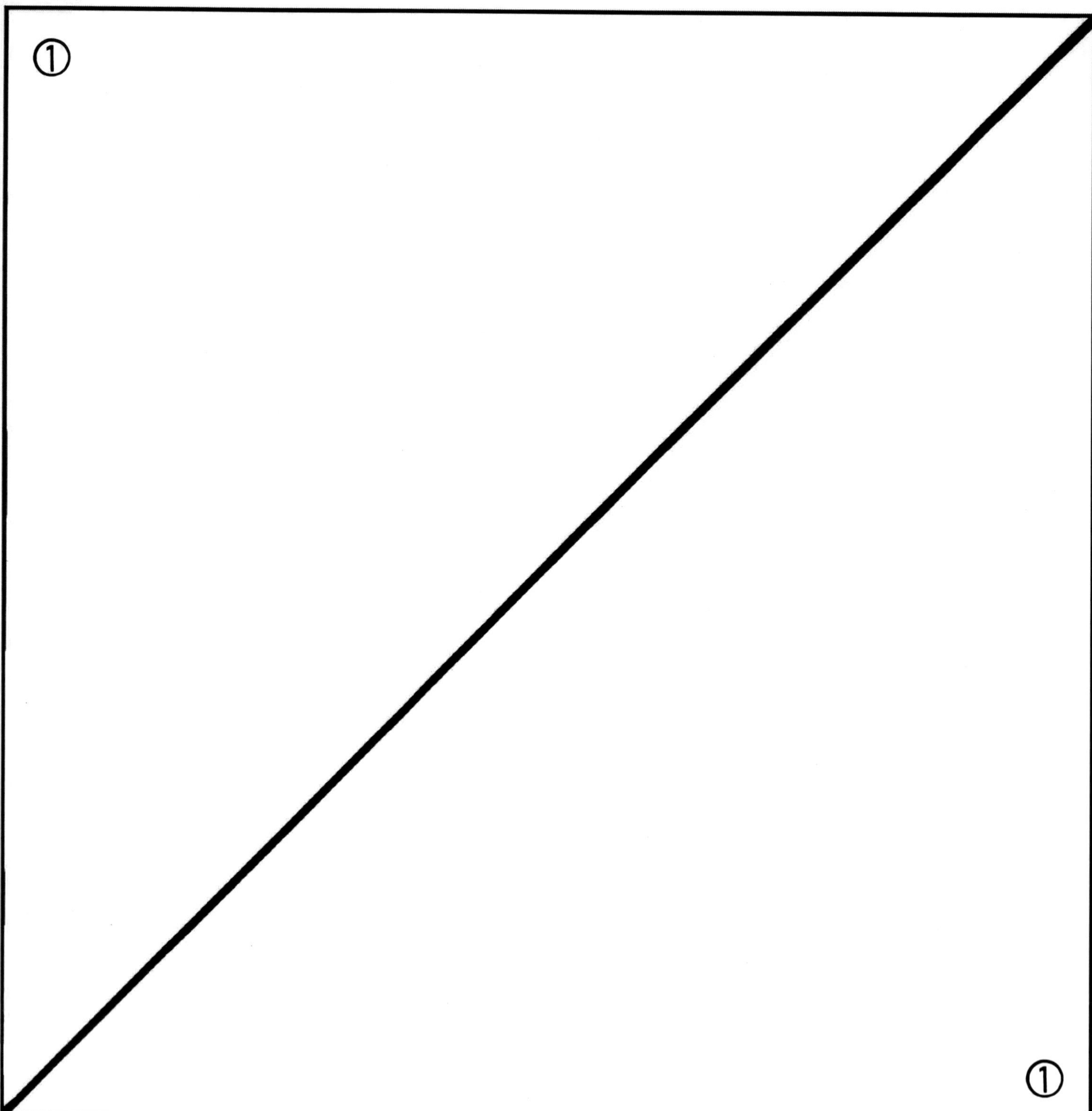
①
①

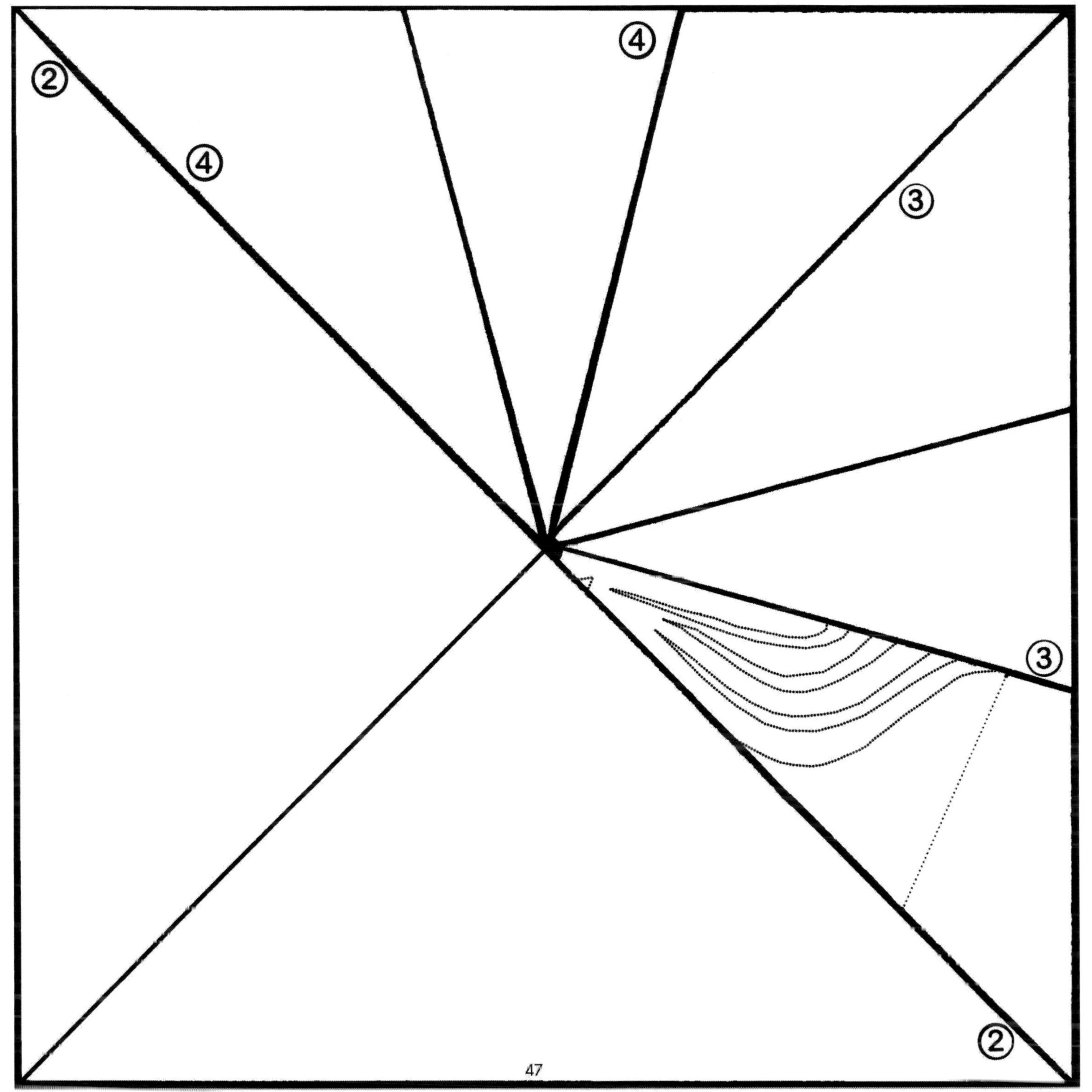
②
④
④
③
③
②

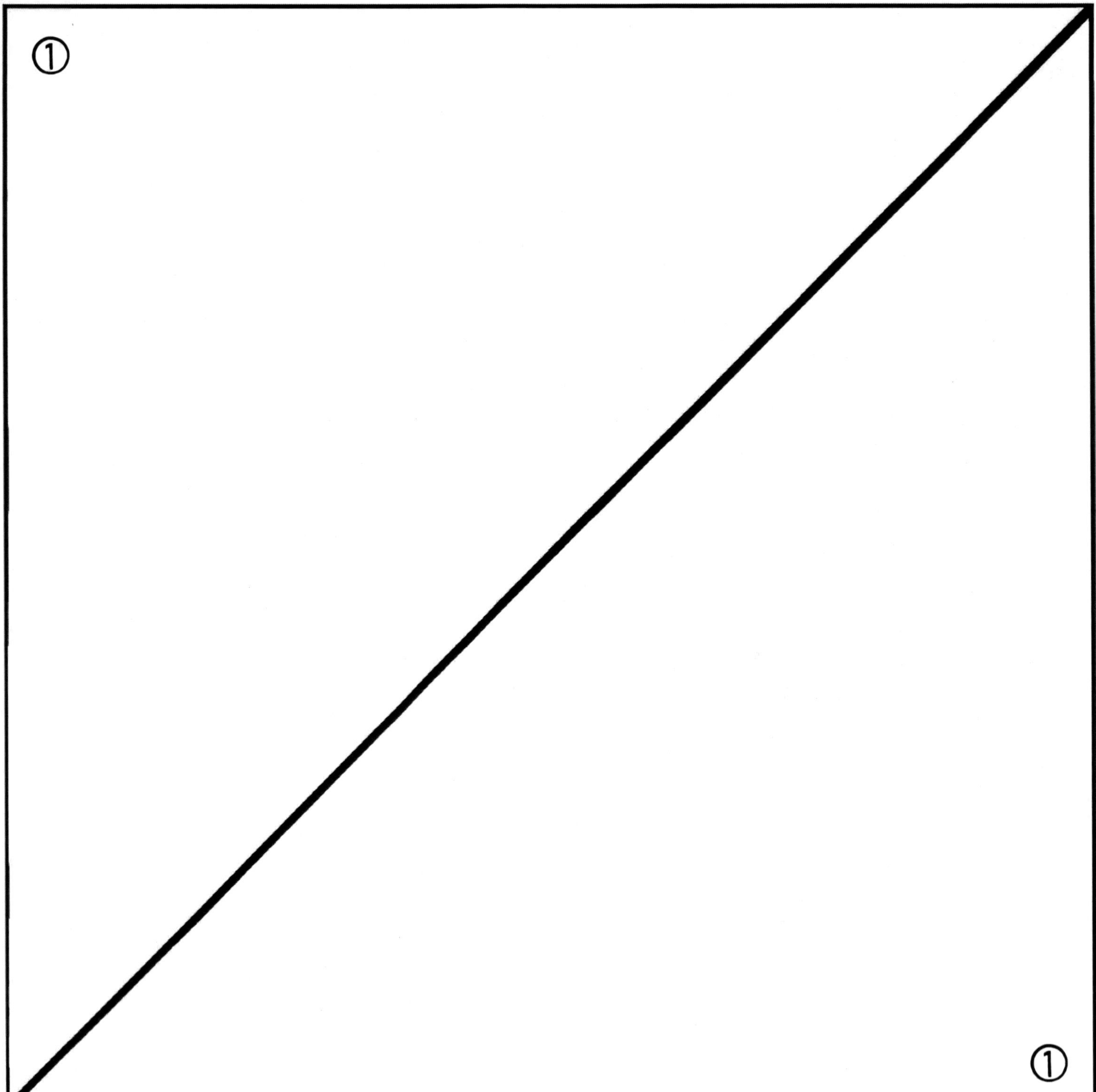

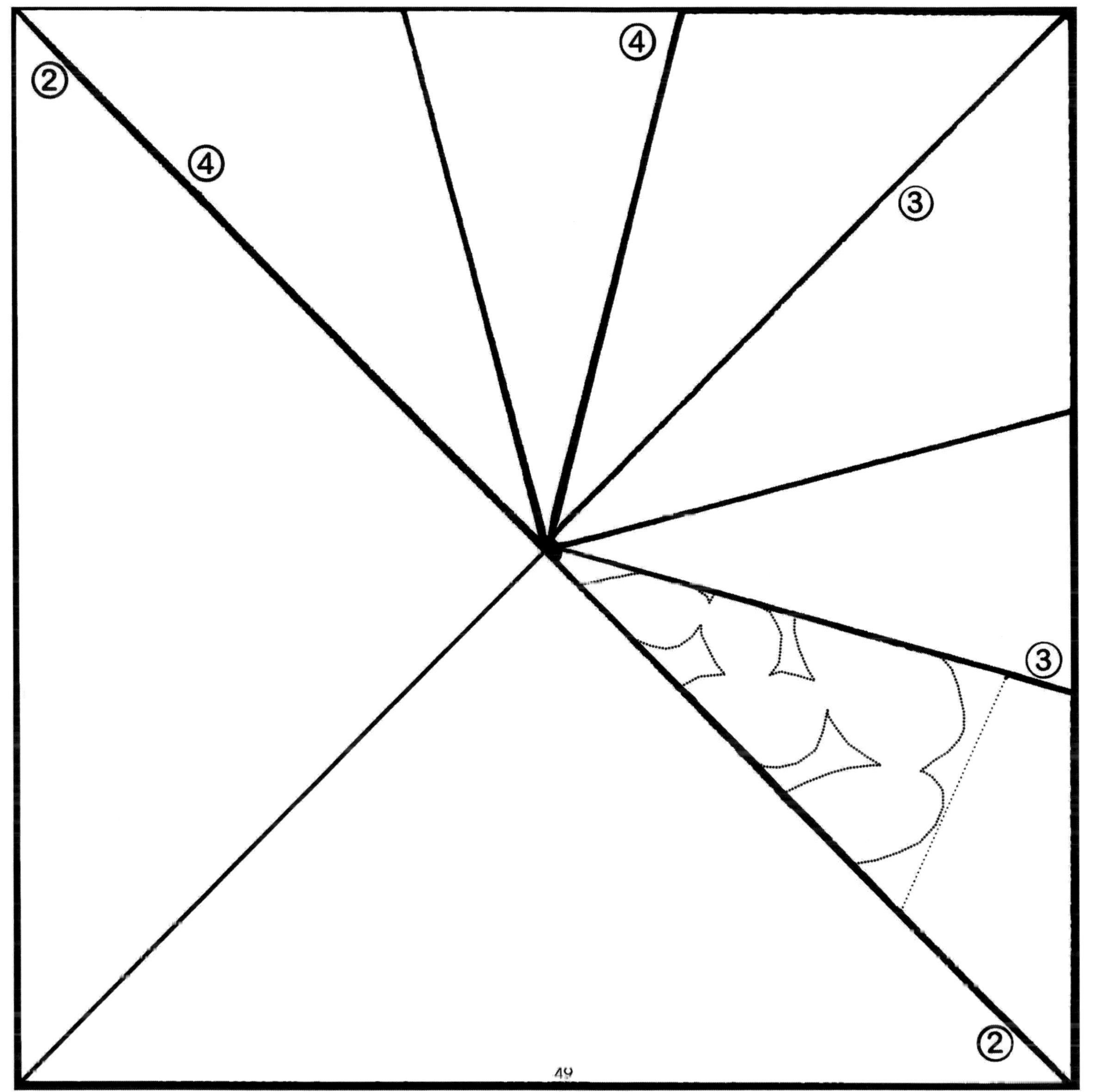
②
④
④
③
③
②

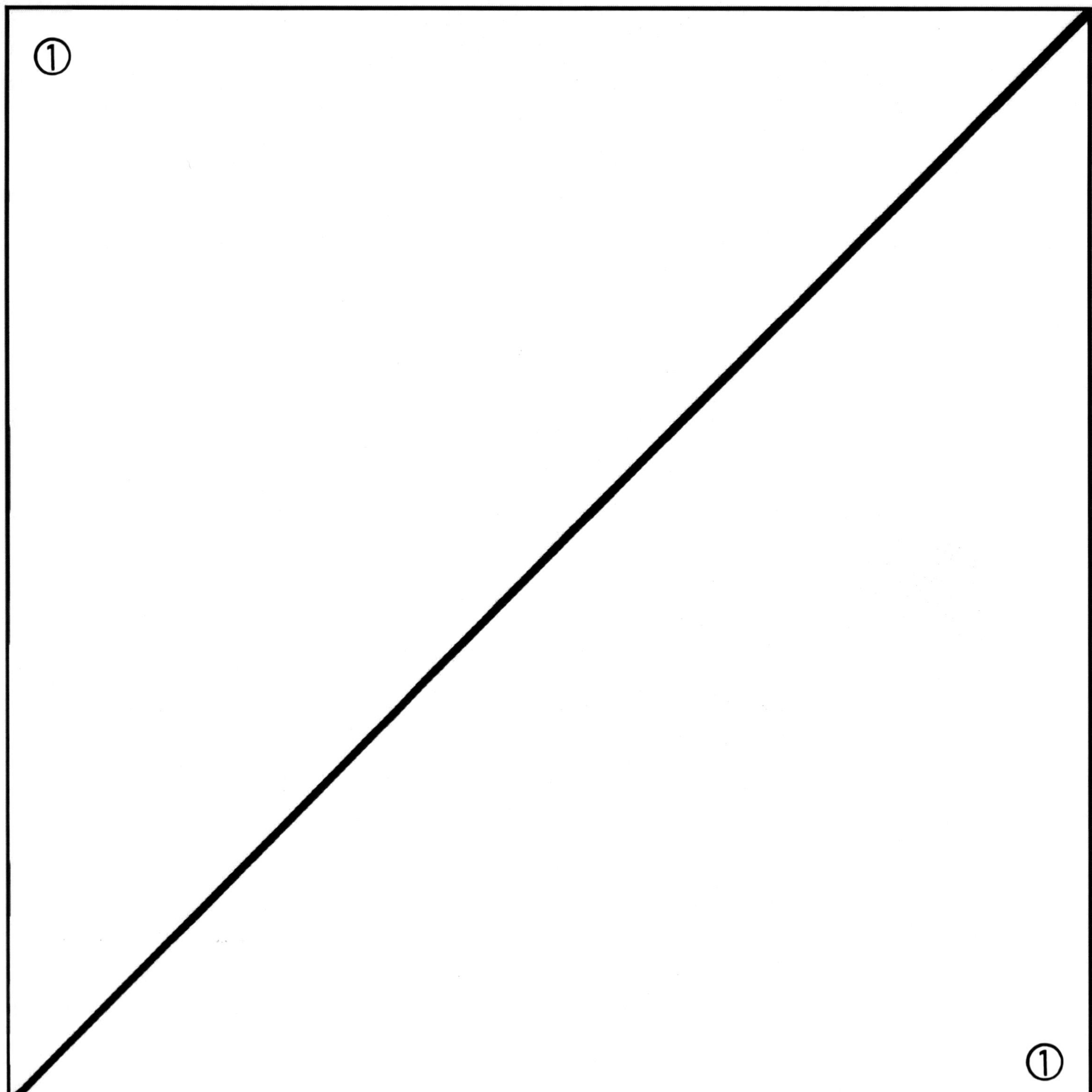
①
①

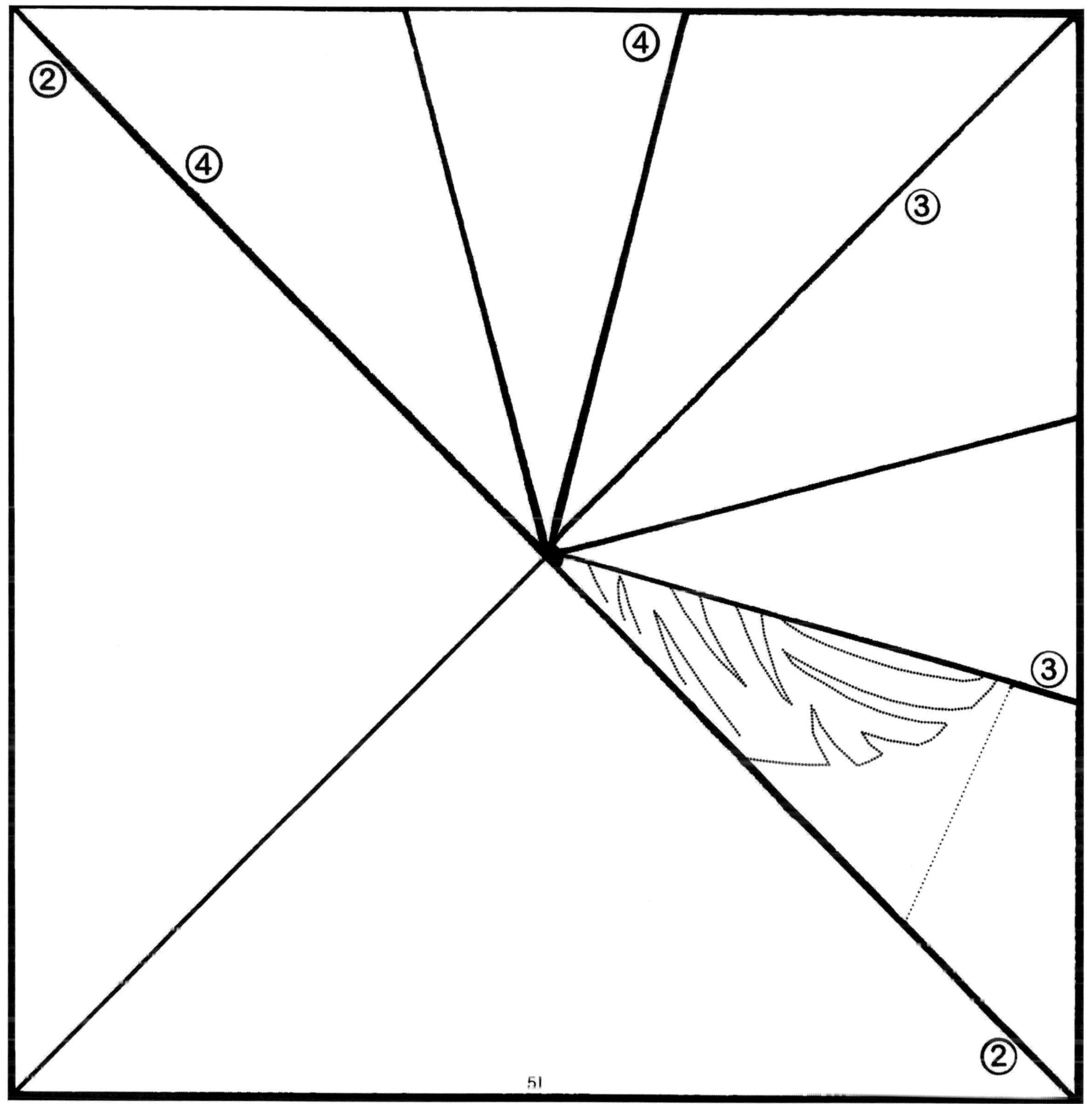
②
④
④
③
③
②

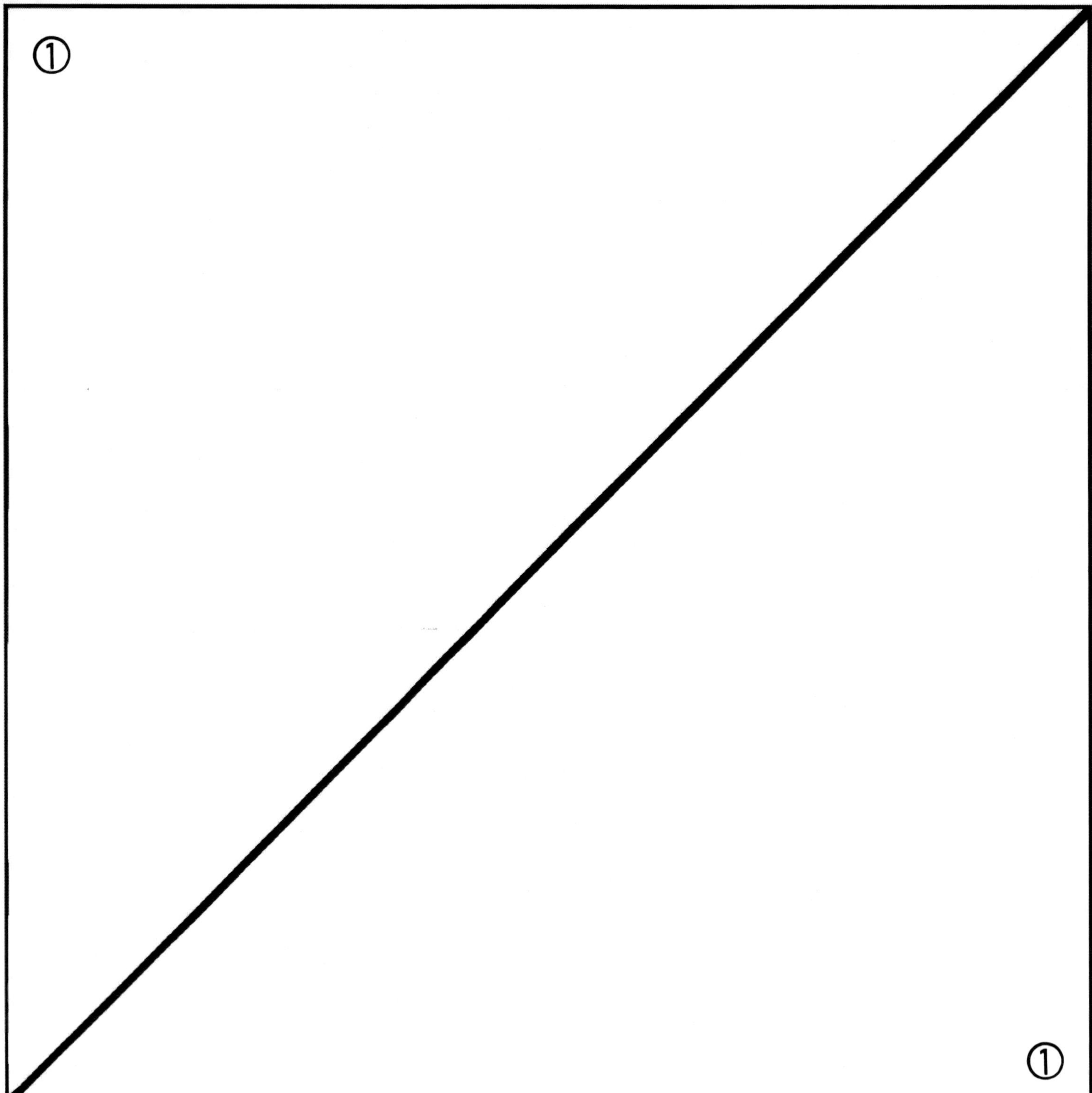
①
①

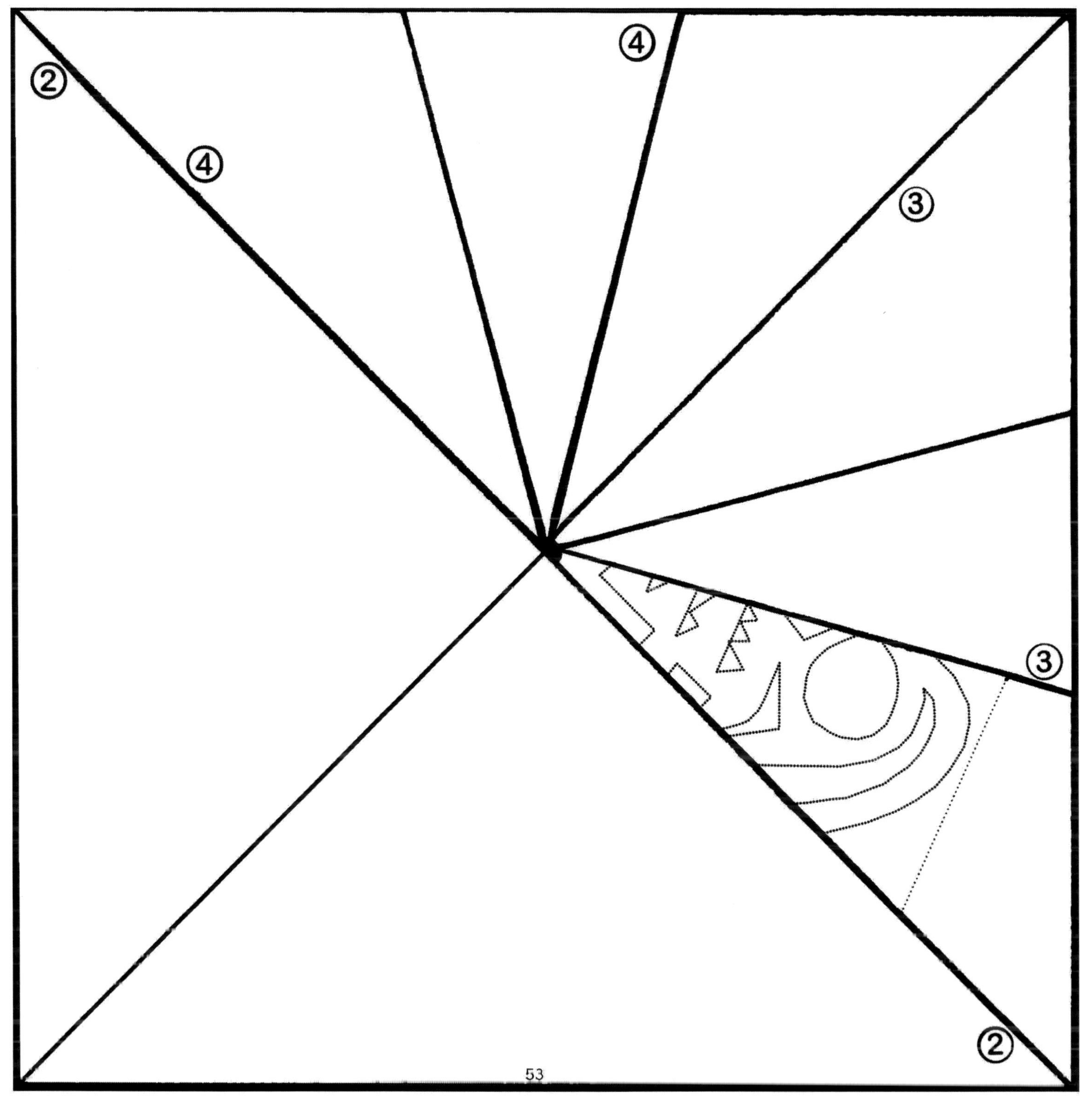
②
④
④
③
③
②

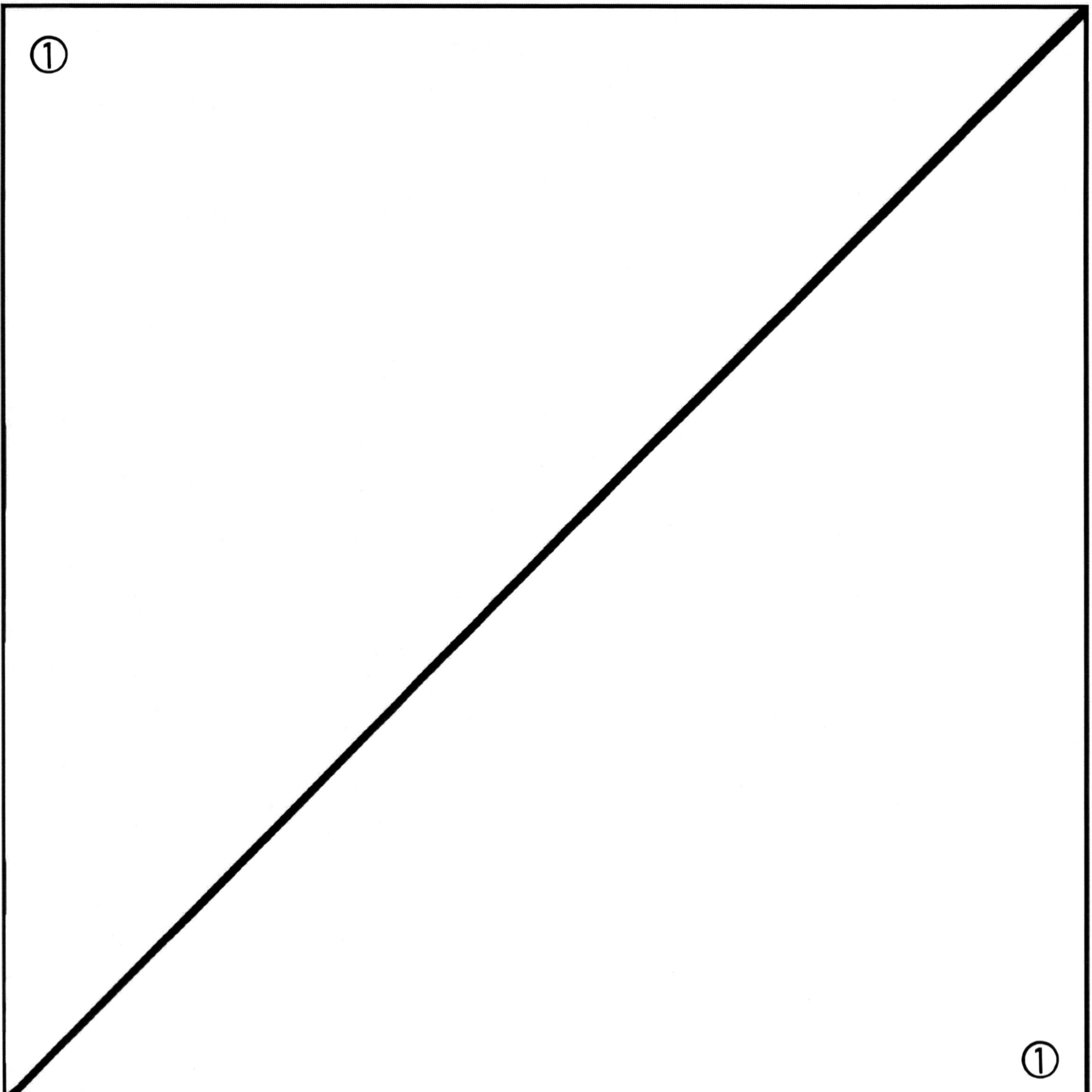
①
①

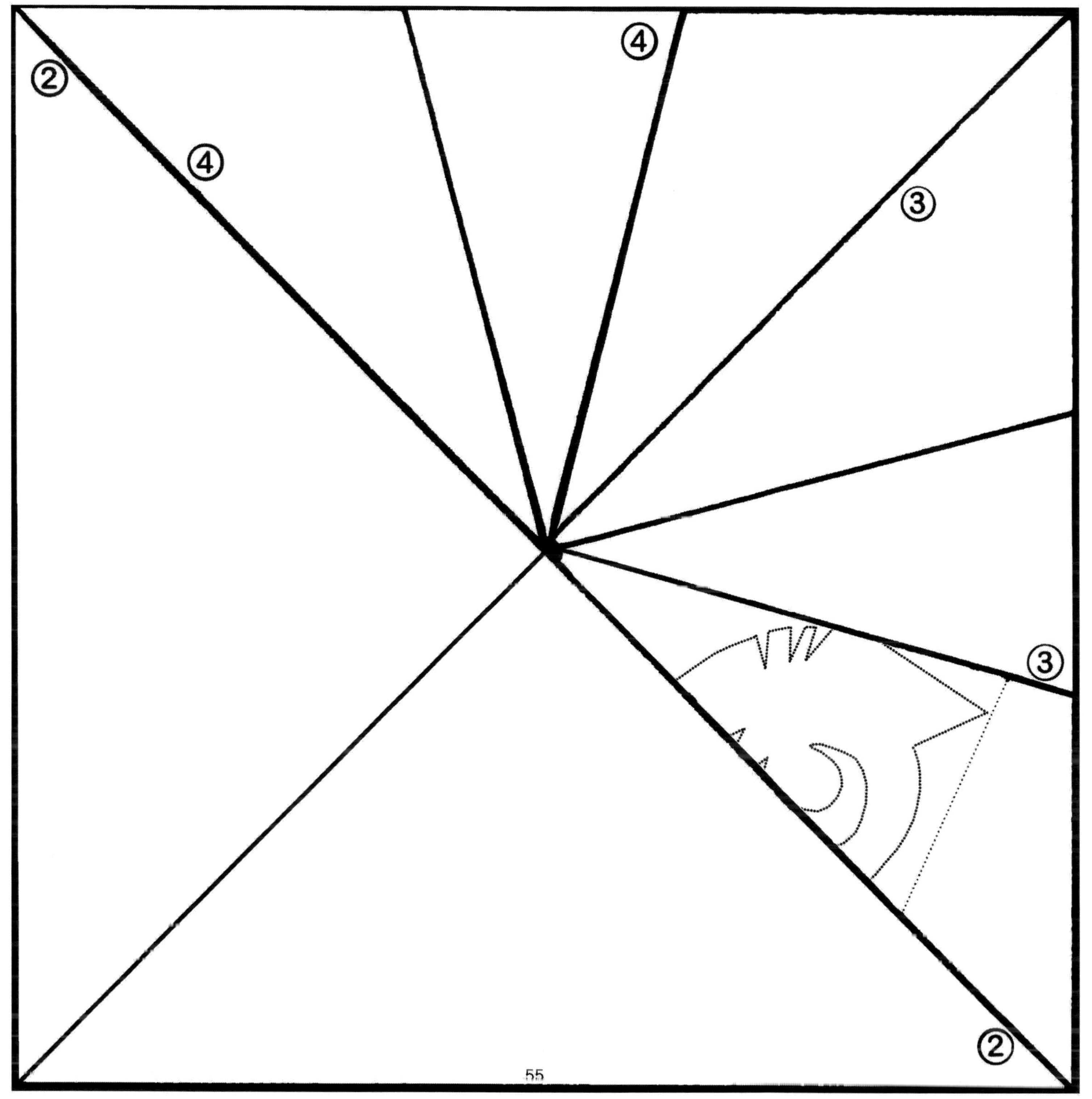
②
④
④
③
③
②

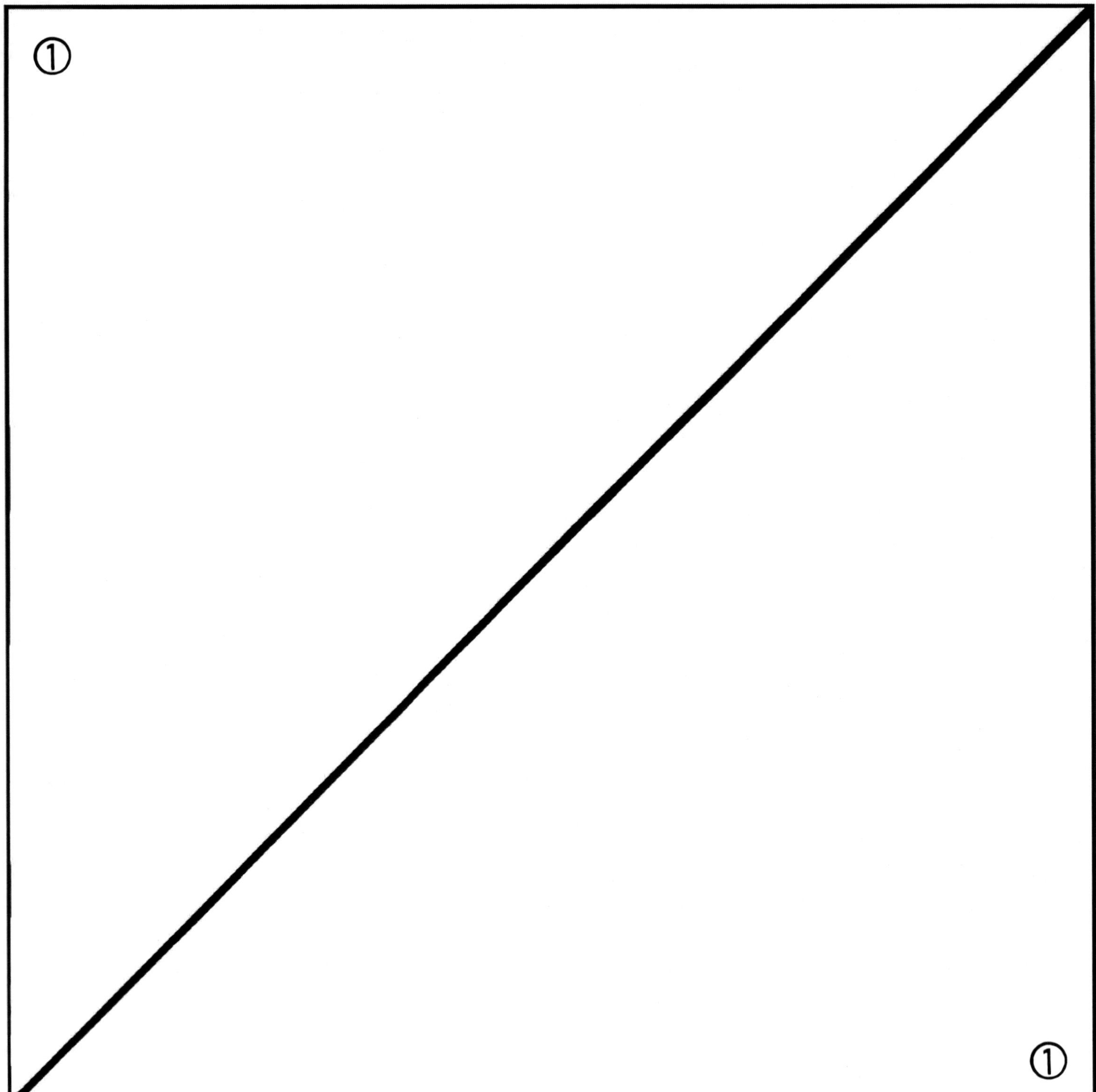
①
①

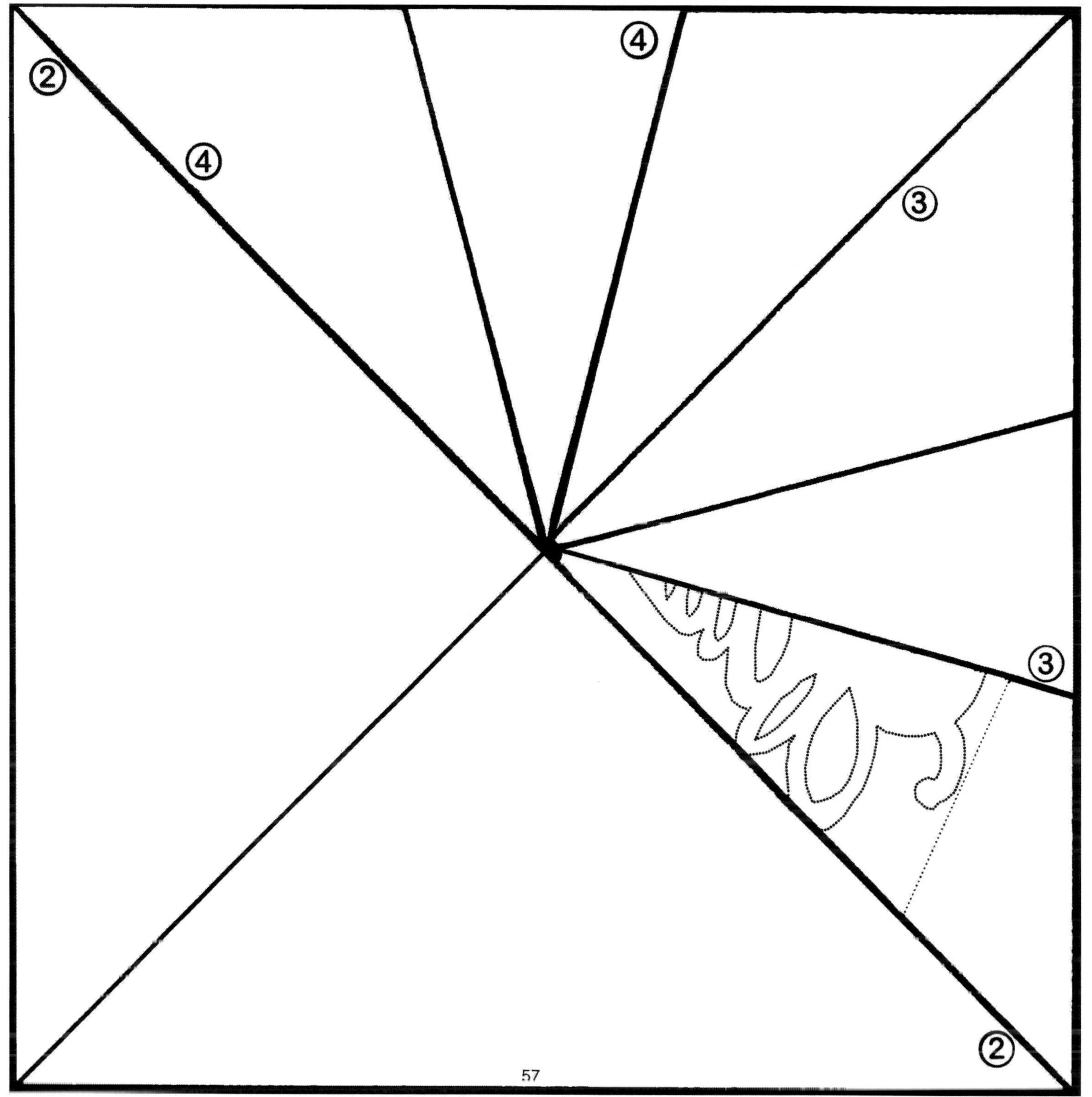
②
④
④
③
③
②

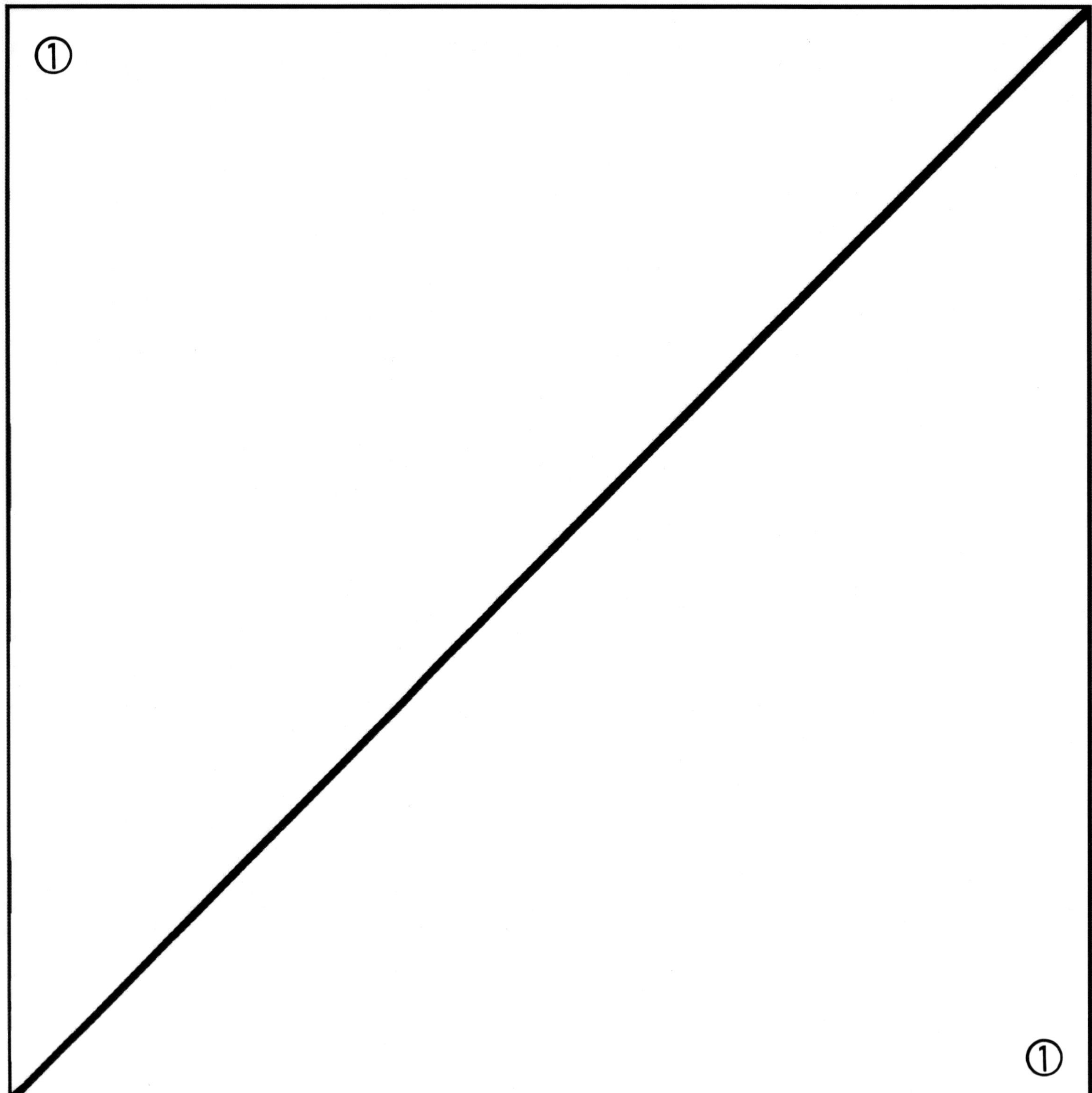
①
①

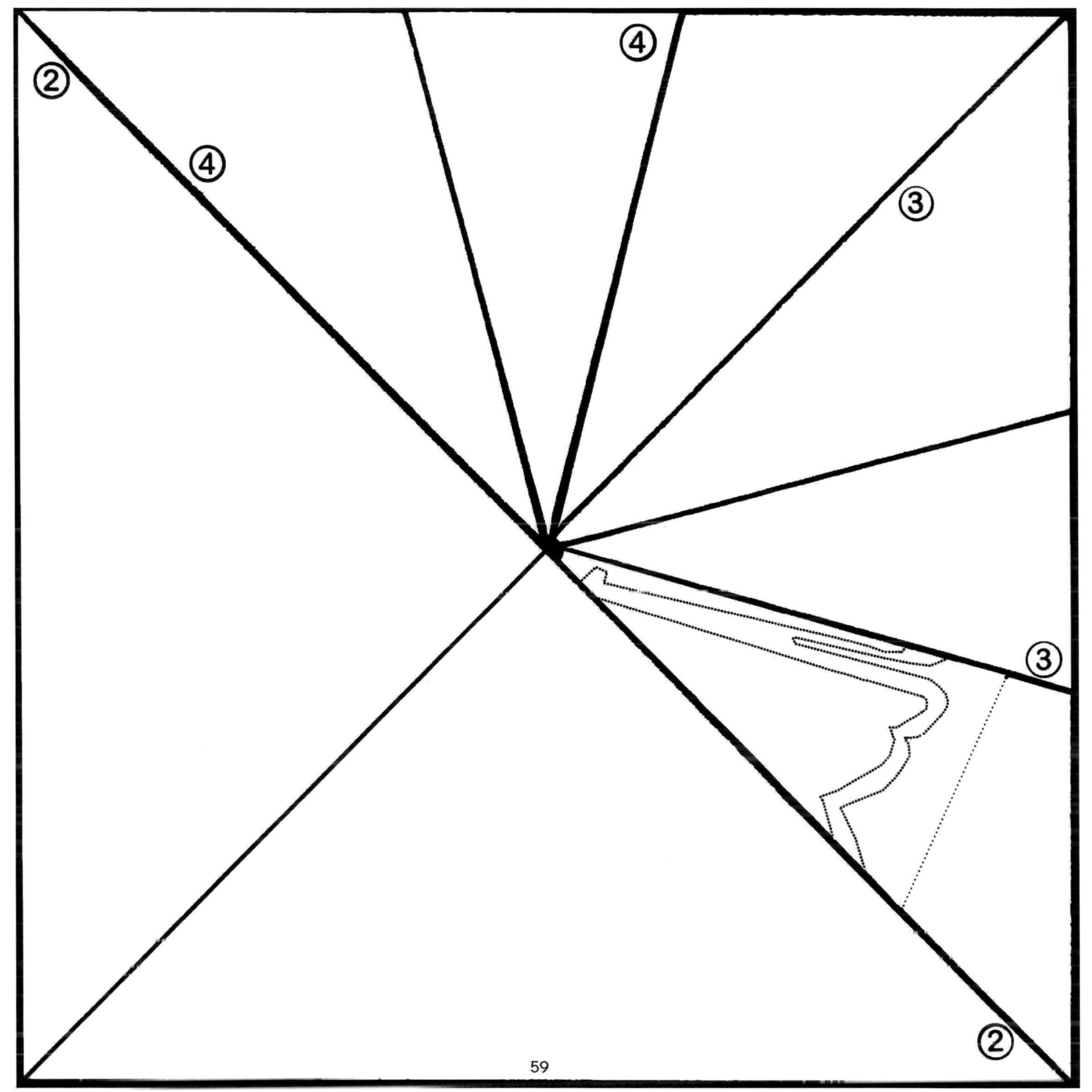
②
④
④
③
③
②

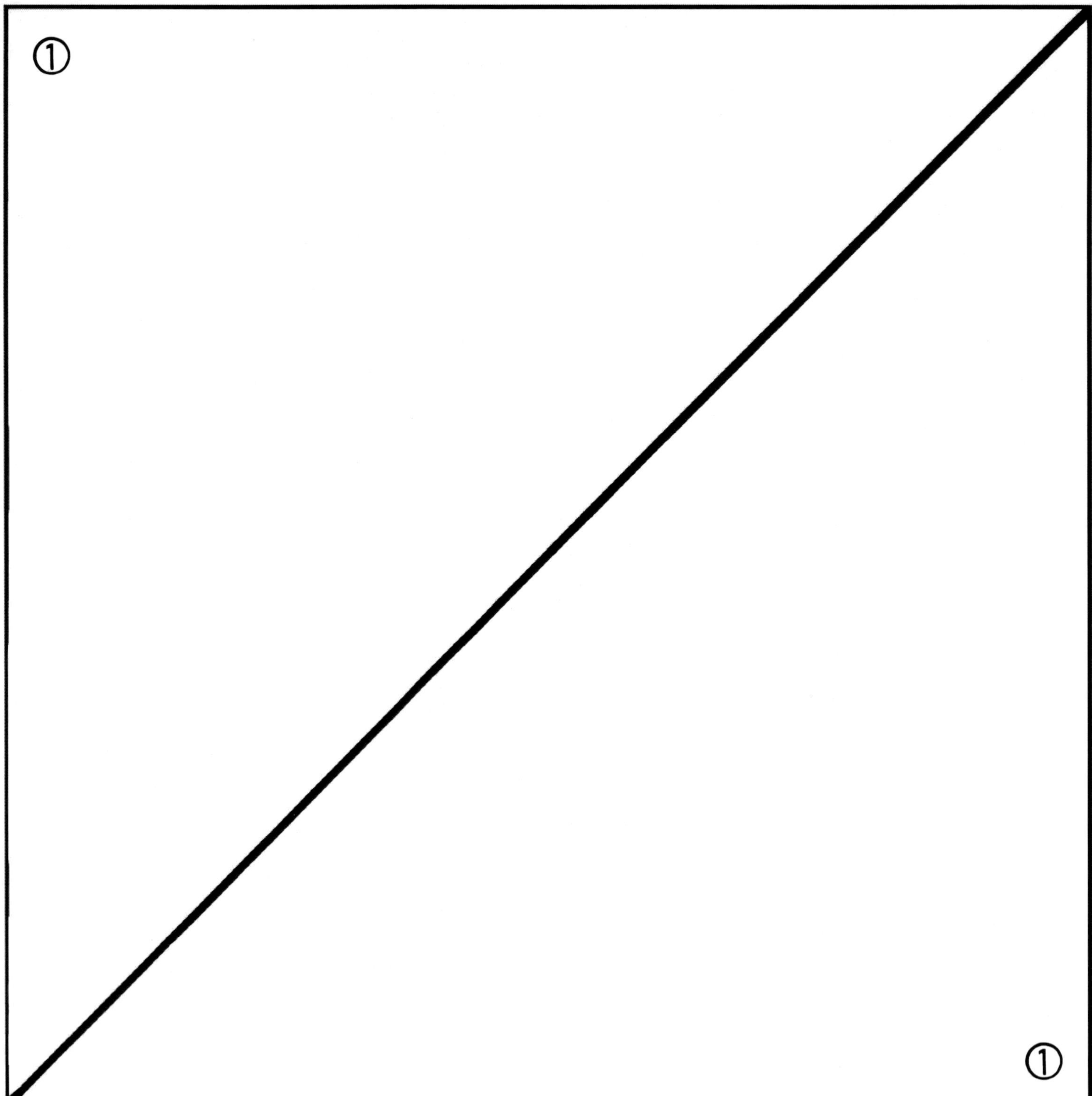
①
①

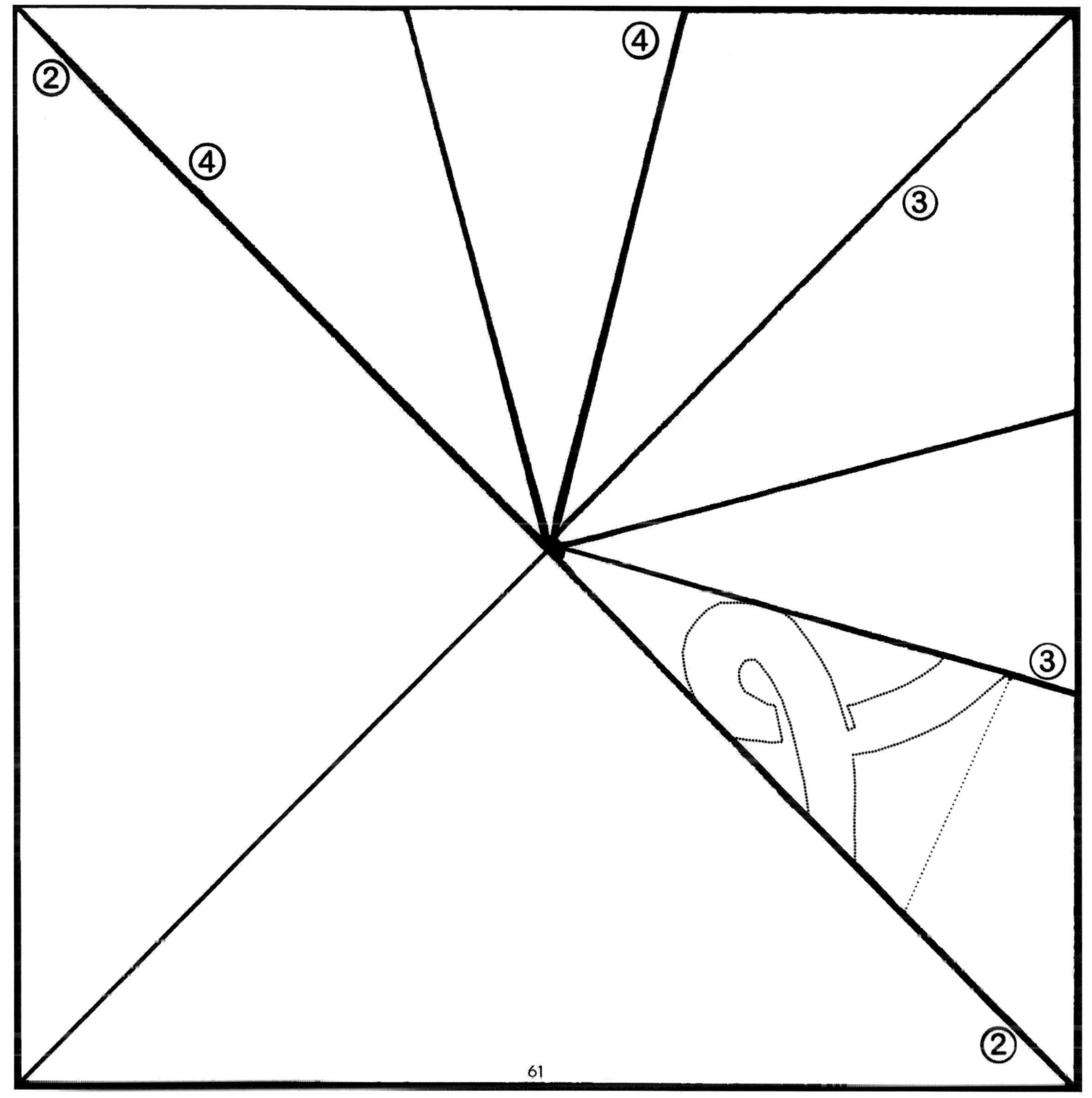
②
④
④
③
③
②

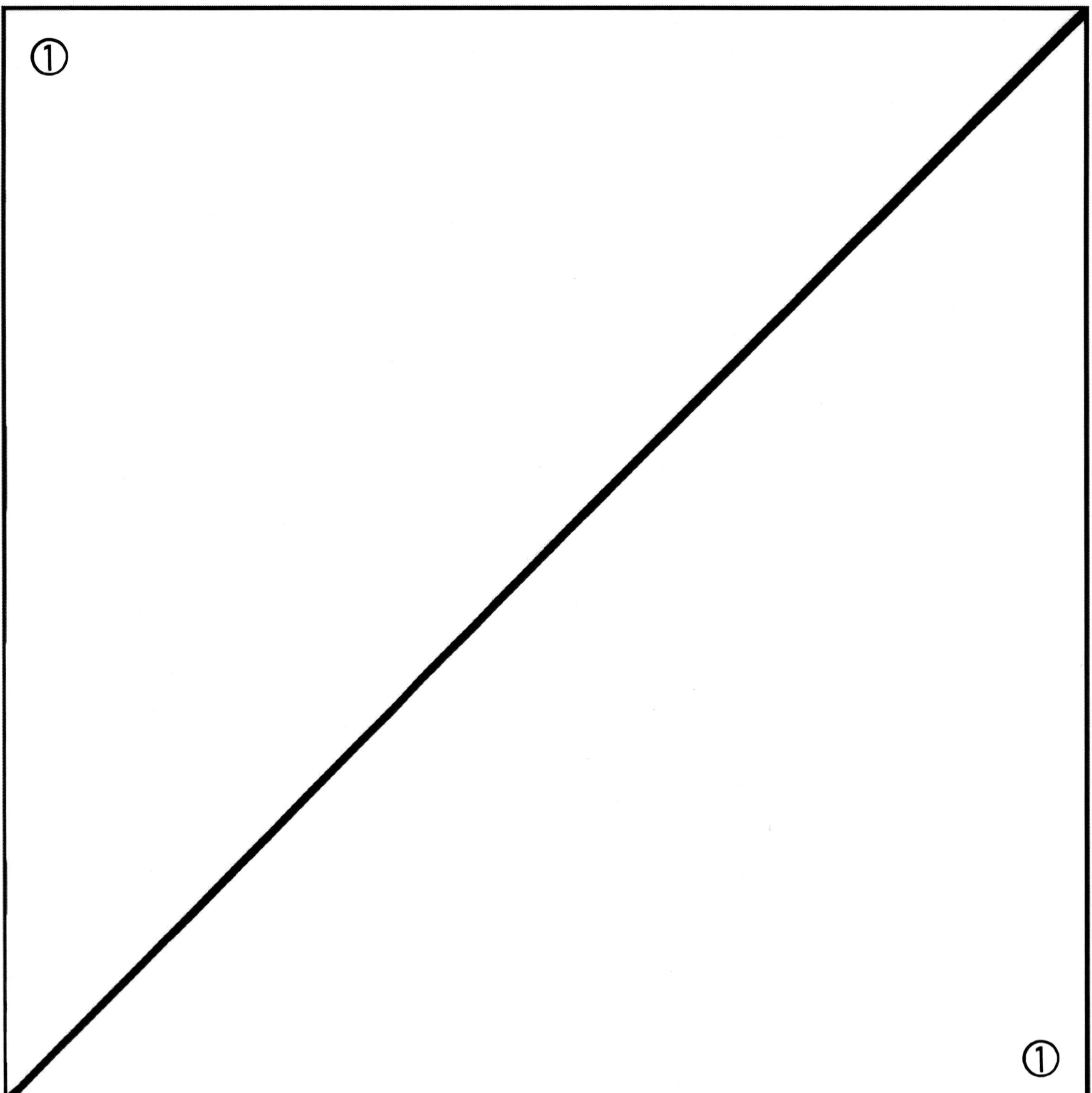
①
①

DESIGNING YOUR OWN SNOWFLAKES

Designing your own snowflakes is my favourite part of the process. I encourage you to give it a try. Here are a few tips:

- There's only one rule to making snowflakes: don't cut completely through both edges! There needs to be a little bit of paper connecting one edge to the next. If you completely cut off both sides of your snowflake panel, your snowflake will fall apart. Don't worry if this happens just grab a new sheet of paper and try again. Sometimes, you can salvage the snowflake with some tape.
- Start with some simple shapes. The first few snowflake templates in this book are a great way to start. Try the Single Flower (page 15), Diagonal Star (page 13), and Star Chain (page 19) templates. Simple shapes give you a good idea of how patterns on the folded panel will look when unfolded. They are also easy to cut out!

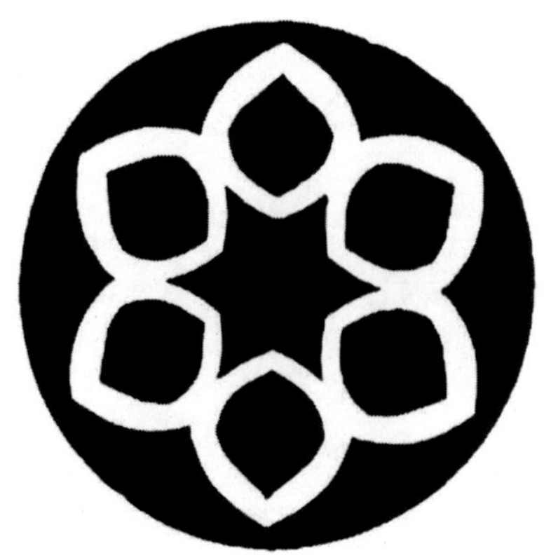

- **Layer simple shapes.** A great next step is to try layering simple shapes. You can practice this by following the Double Flower (page 35) and the Triple Flower (page 37) templates. These templates layer semi-circles to create increasingly complex flowers. Try this with any shape! Some of my favourites are semi-circles, hearts, triangles and stars.

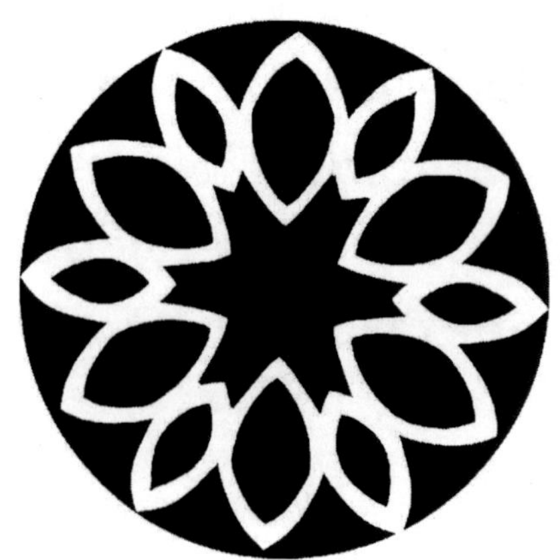

- **Consider negative space.** Negative space is the empty space left from cut away paper. Designs created from negative space can be just as beautiful and interesting as designs on paper. If you follow the Zig-zag template (page 31), you can create the same snowflake twice: once in positive space and once in negative space.
- **Remember symmetry.** Snowflakes have many axes of symmetry. These include halves, quarters, and twelfths. The Owl template uses the twelfths axis to create the silhouette of an owl. Other examples include the Butterfly (page 39) and Cat (page 55) templates. Experiment with different axes of symmetry to see how your designs change!

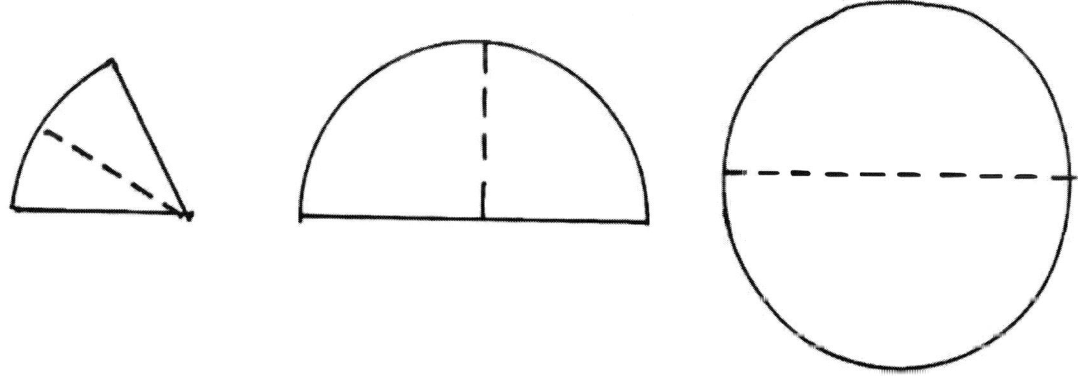

- Try looking at the shapes of household objects. This is my second favourite way to think of snowflake designs! In the past, I've used vitamin bottles, chess pieces, spoons, cereal boxes, bracelets and more as inspiration for snowflakes. The Diamond (page 25) template was inspired by my kitchen table! Rather than trying to make my snowflake look exactly like an object, I usually have more fun if I focus on the abstract line the object creates in space.

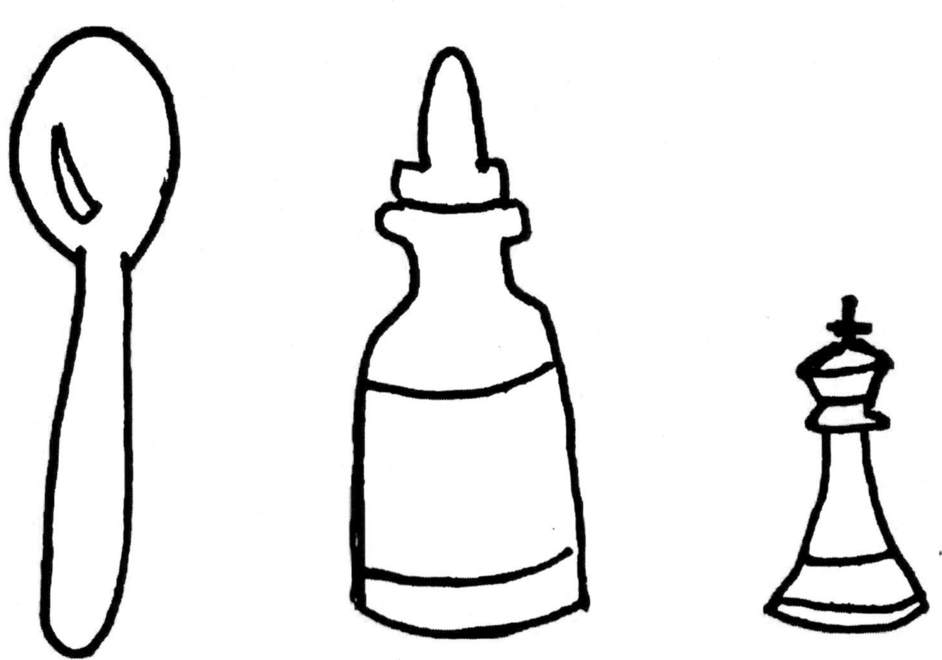

- Try other folding techniques! While twelve panels creates a nice balance to the finished snowflake, there are many other ways to fold paper. Try folding halves, quarters, thirds, sixths, eighths, and sixteenths using what you learned in HOW TO FOLD THE PAPER FOR SNOWFLAKES.

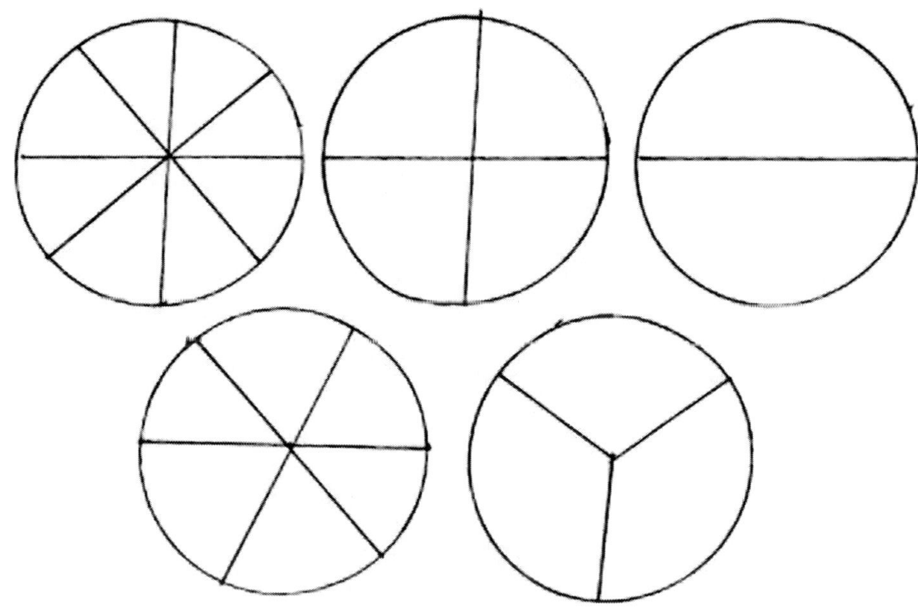

- **Don't be afraid to freehand!** My favourite way to design snowflakes is freehand. Don't think too hard about where or how you cut, just start creating shapes and see what happens! Some of my favourite designs were created this way, including the Owl (page 53) and the Swan (page 39).

- **Have fun!** This book is a guide, not a textbook. Don't worry about creating designs that look exactly like the ones in this book. Use the techniques and methods in this book to create your own designs. I am excited to see what you create!

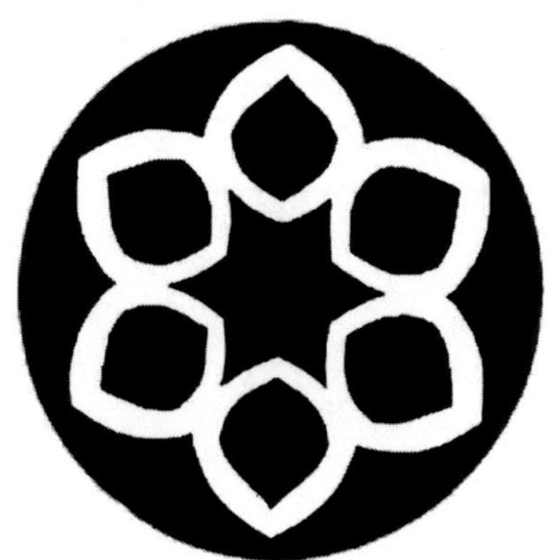

BLANK TEMPLATES

Use these blank templates to make your own snowflake designs!

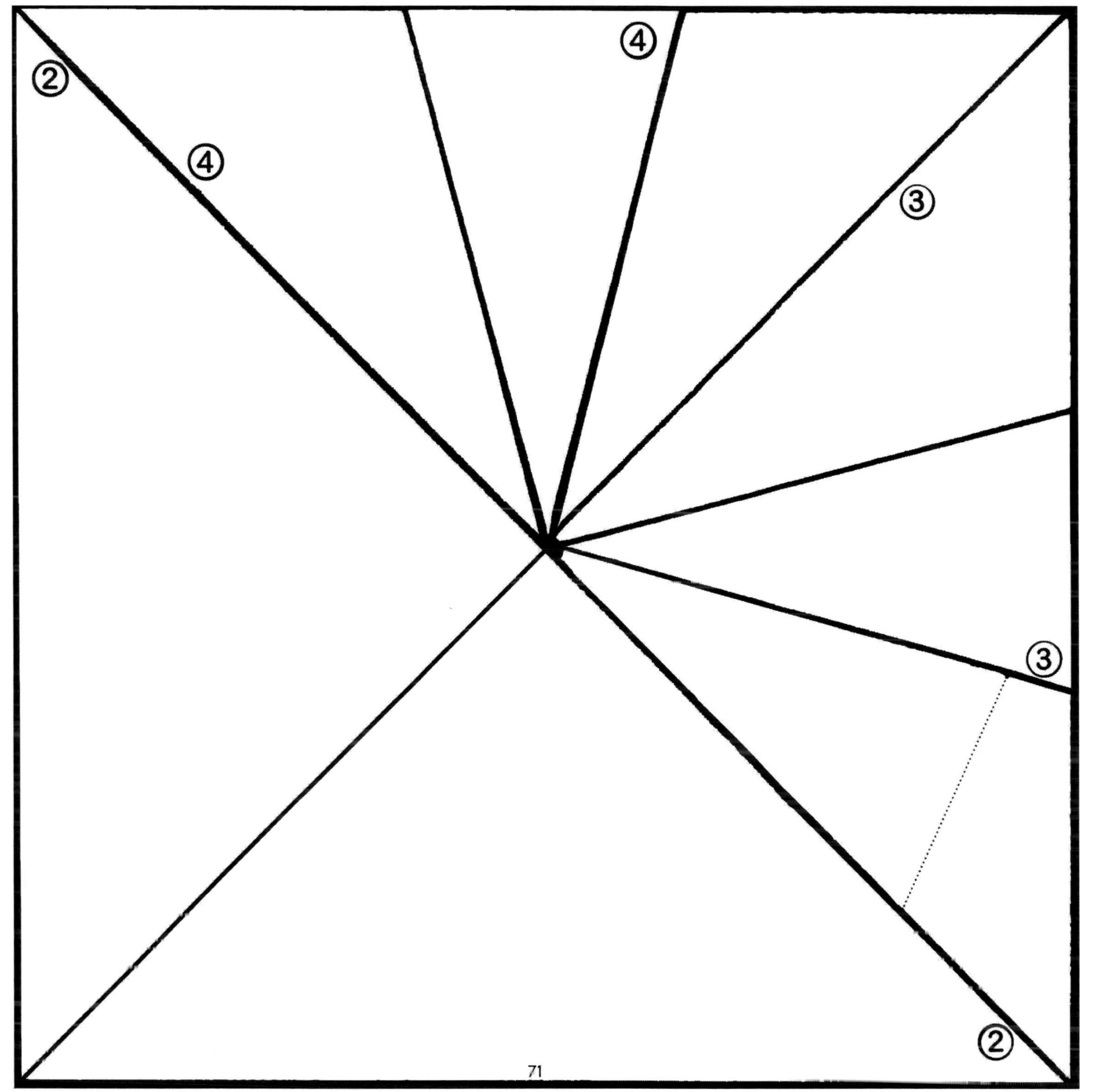
②
④
④
③
③
②

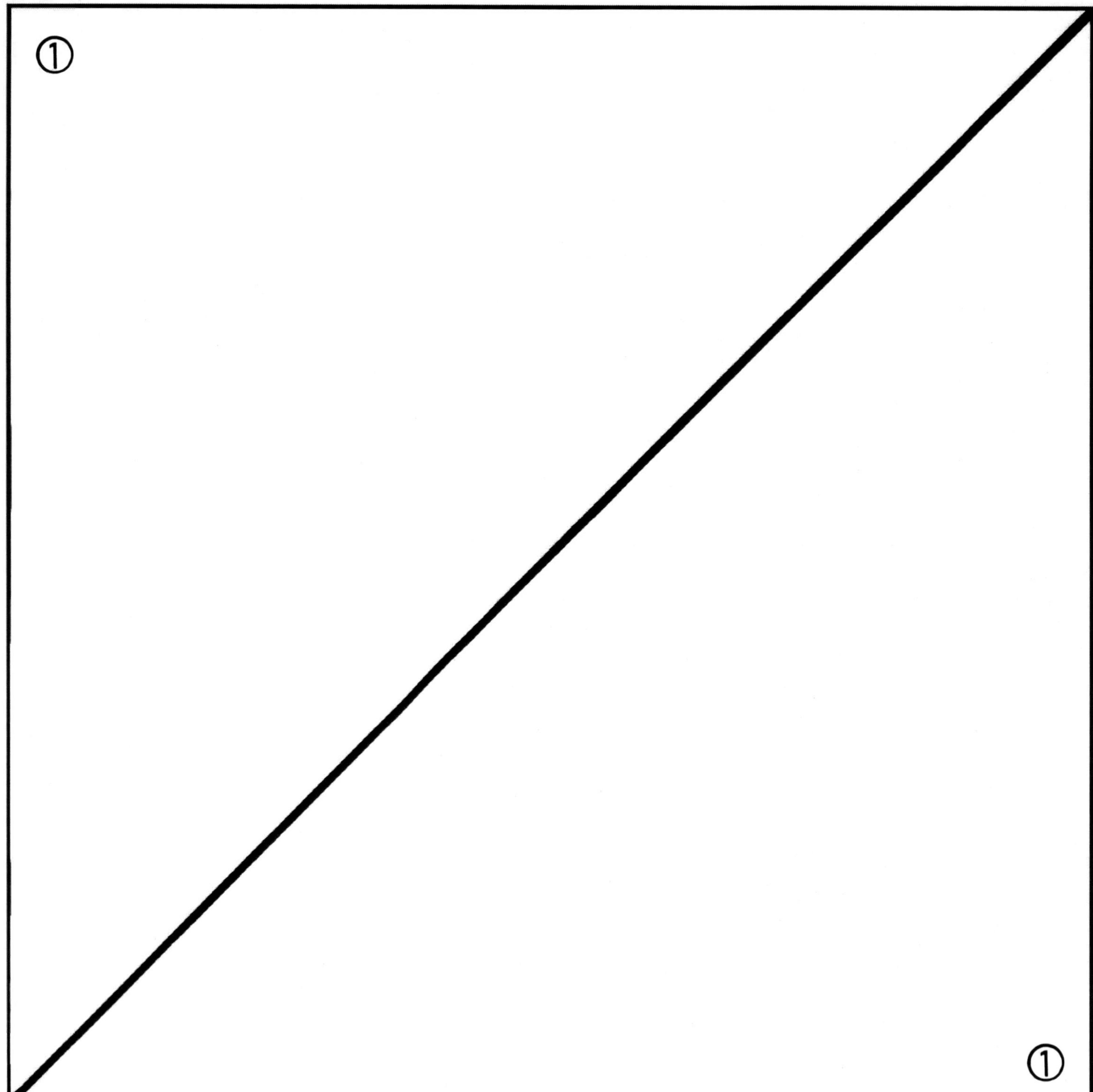
①
①

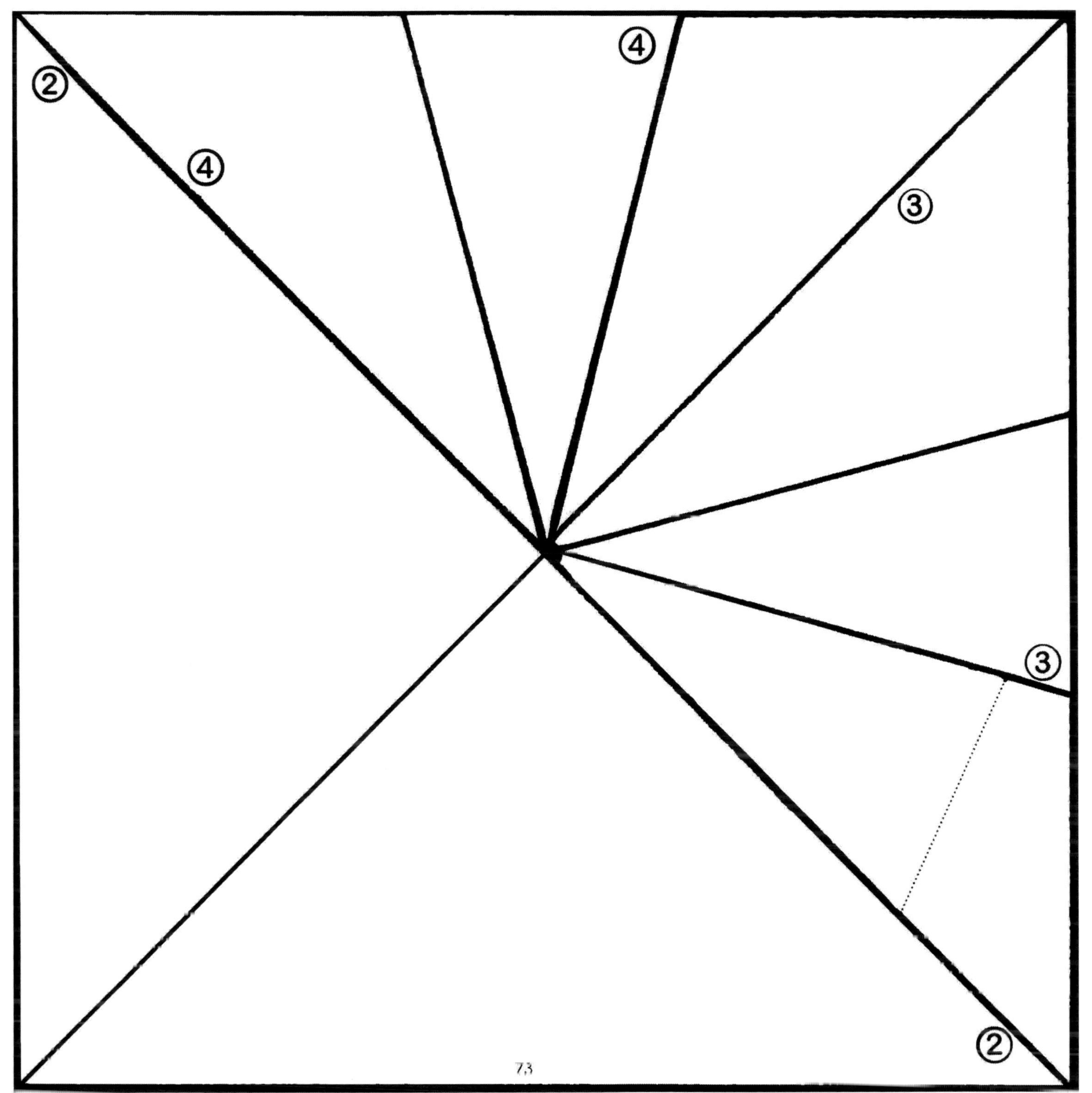
②
④
④
③
③
②

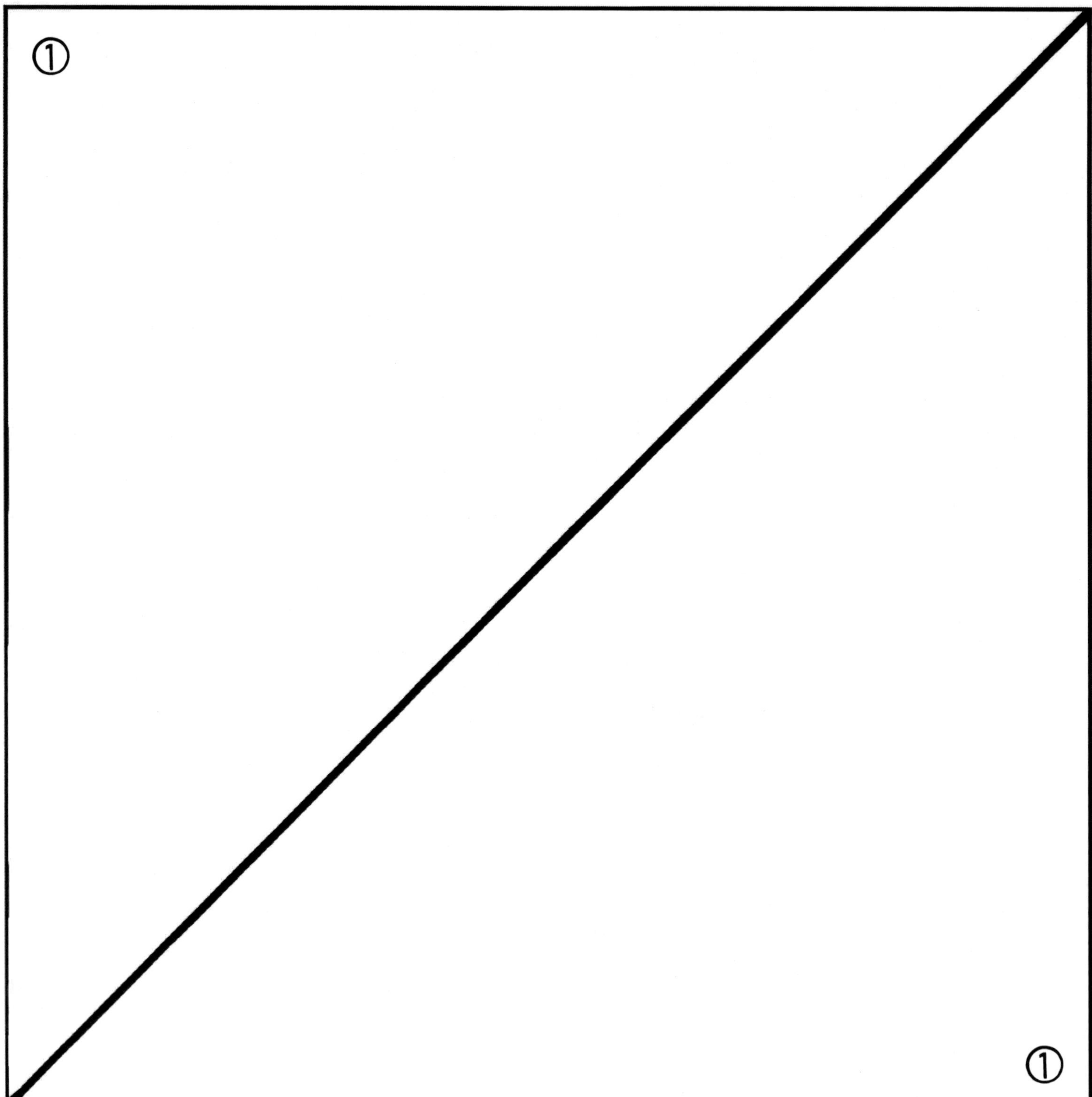
①
①

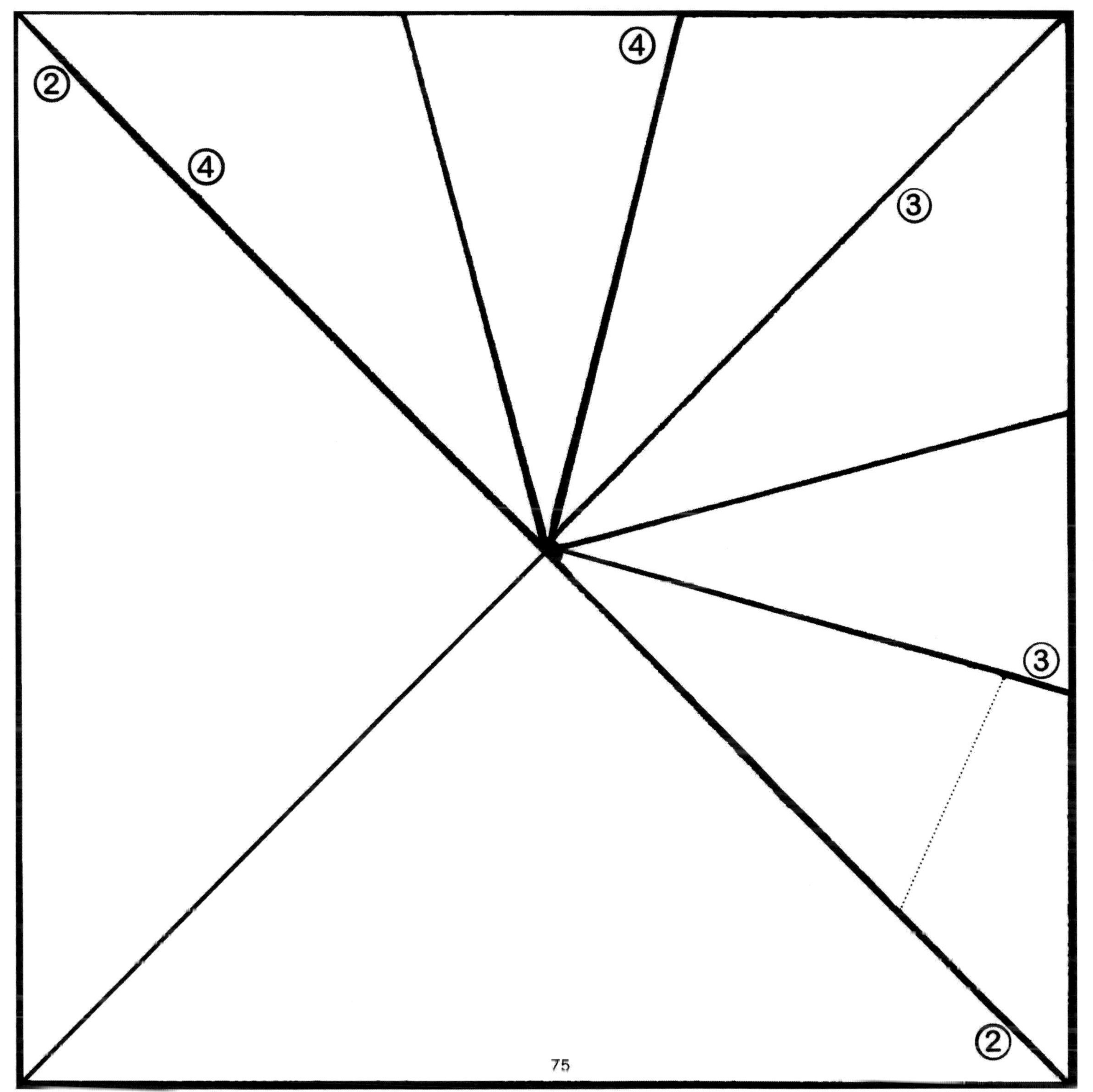
②
④
④
③
③
②

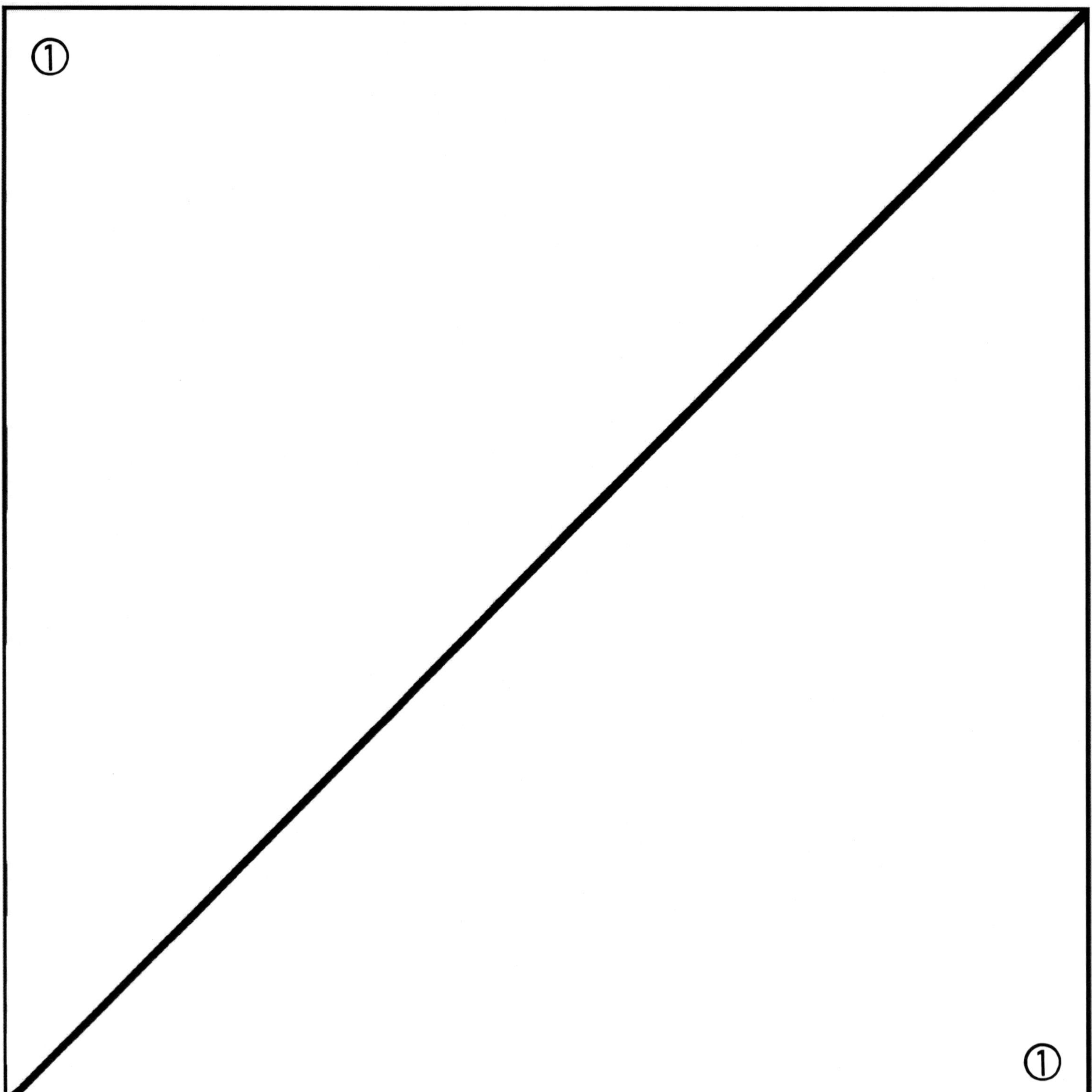
①
①

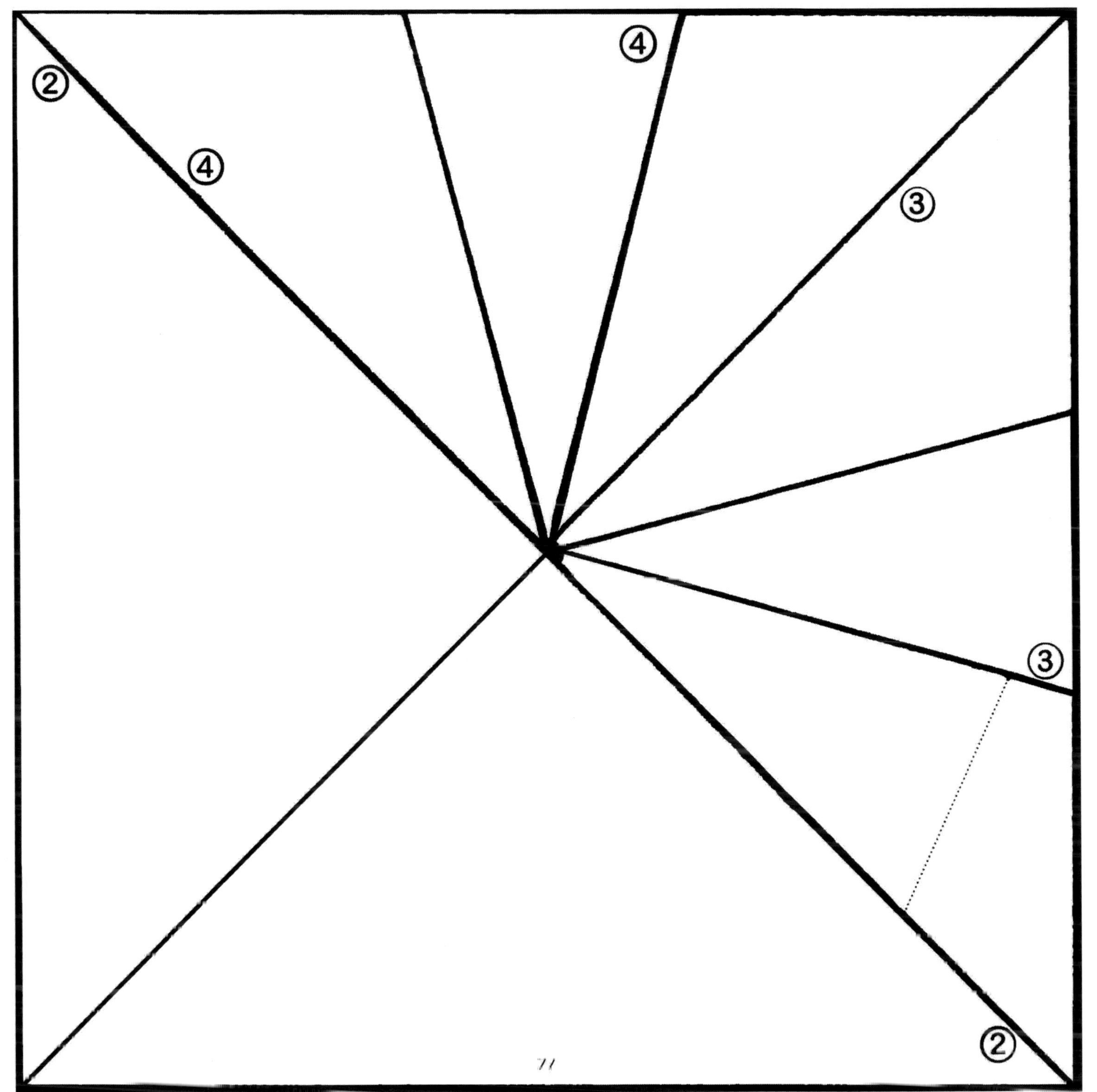
②
④
④
③
③
②

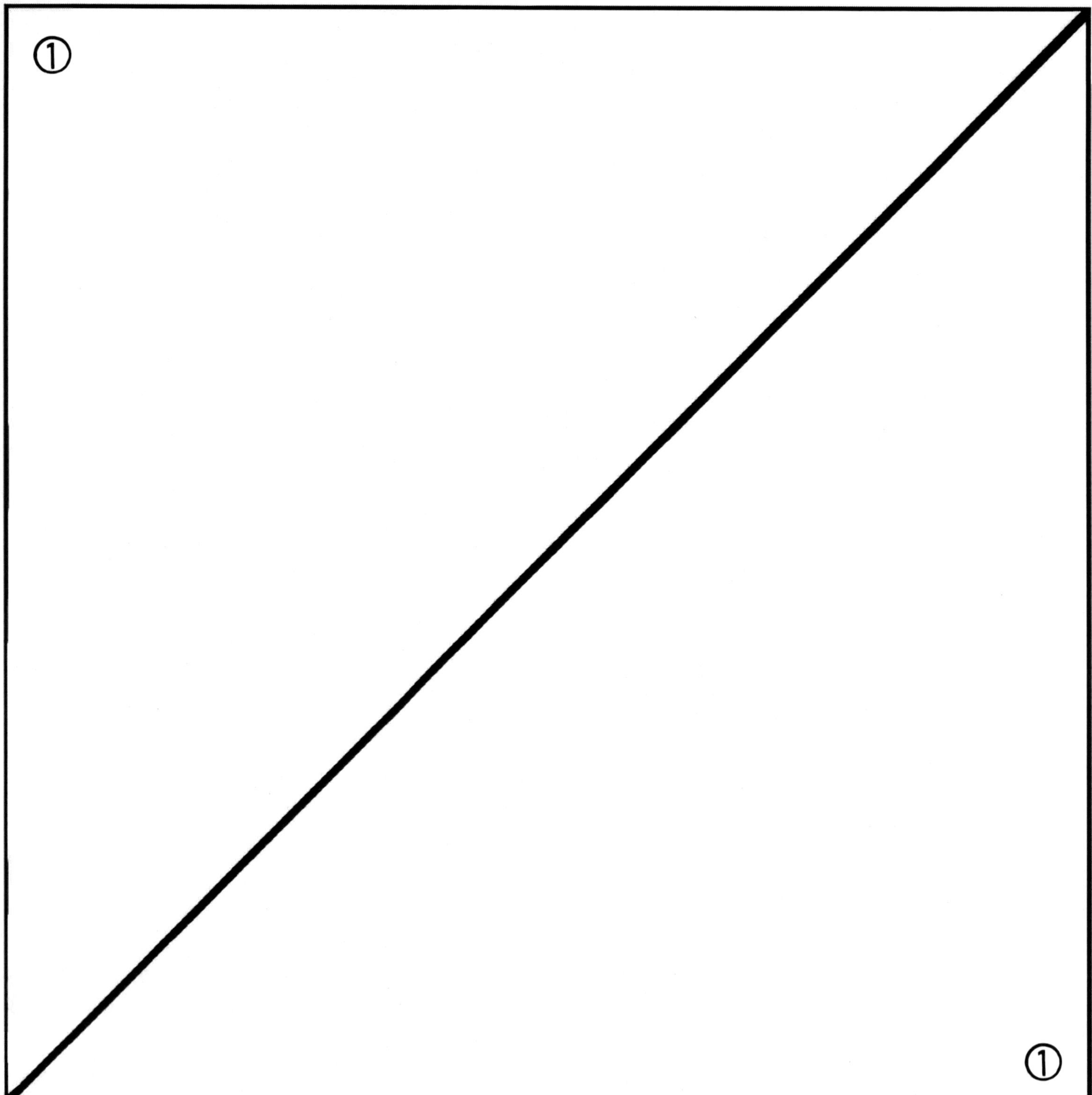
①
①

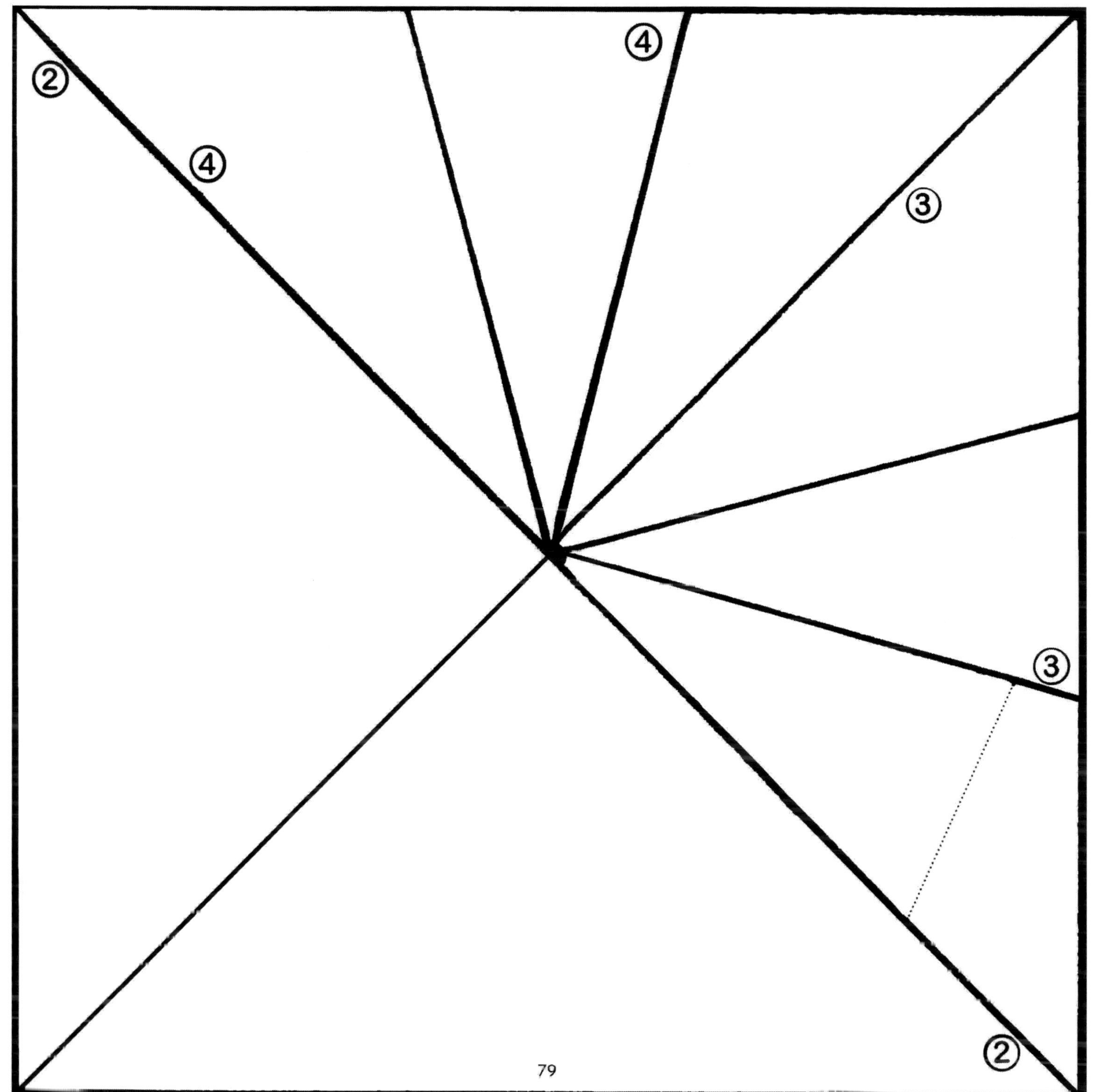
②
④
④
③
③
②

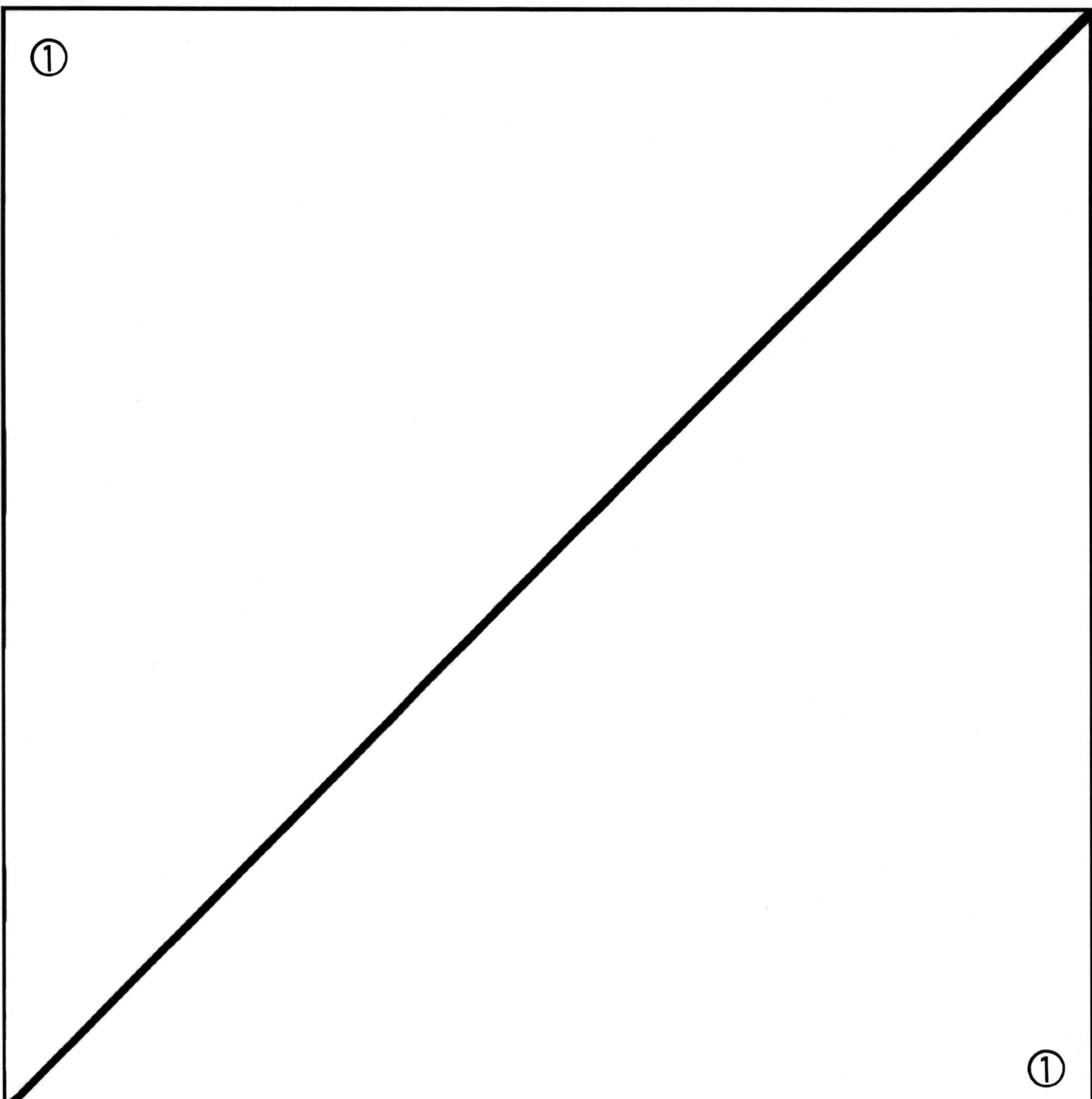
①
①

DISPLAYING YOUR SNOWFLAKES

What can you do with your snowflakes once they are finished? If satisfying your creative itch isn't enough, here are some ideas for how to use finished snowflakes:

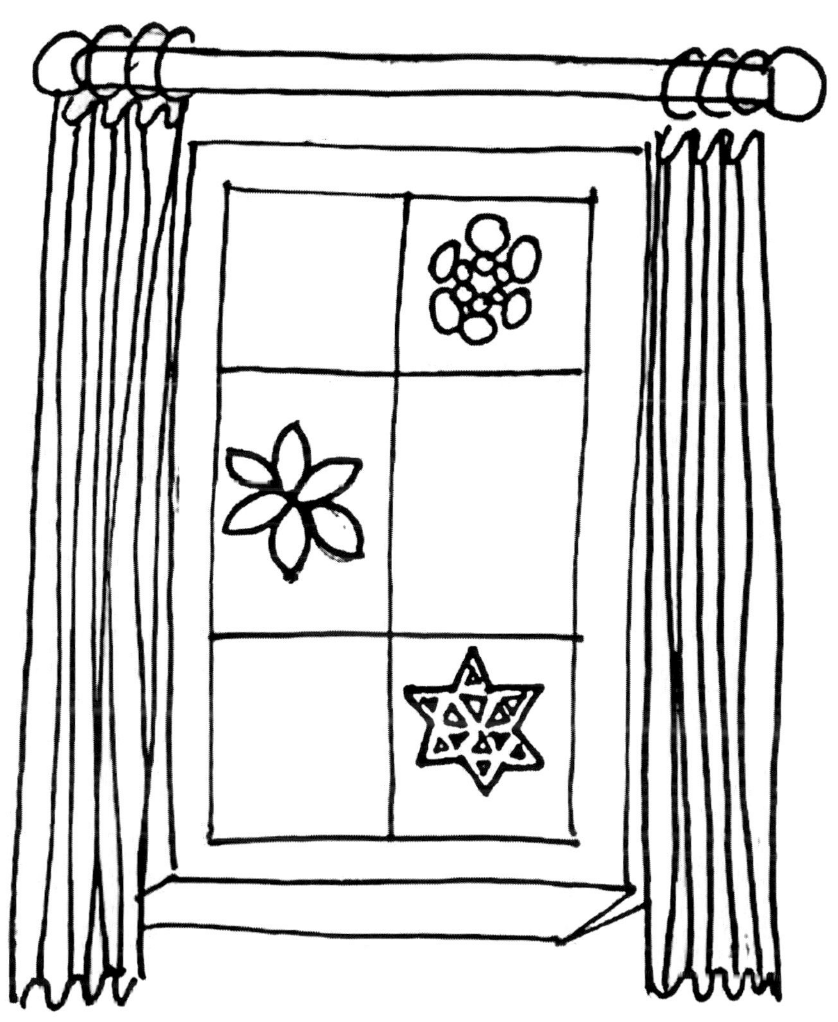

- **Hang them in the window.** This is a classic way to decorate with paper snowflakes. Try using tape, sticky tac, hooks, or string to hang your snowflakes in the window. When the light shines through your windows, it will cast snowflake shadows on your walls!

Make a snowflake garland. First, you will need to make sure your snowflakes lie flat. You can try pressing them under some heavy books for a day, reinforcing them with straws or popsicle sticks, or gluing them to cardstock circles. I usually glue them to cardstock circles. Next, either use a hole punch, staples, or glue to attach each snowflake to a long ribbon. Hang your snowflake garland anywhere you want to display it!

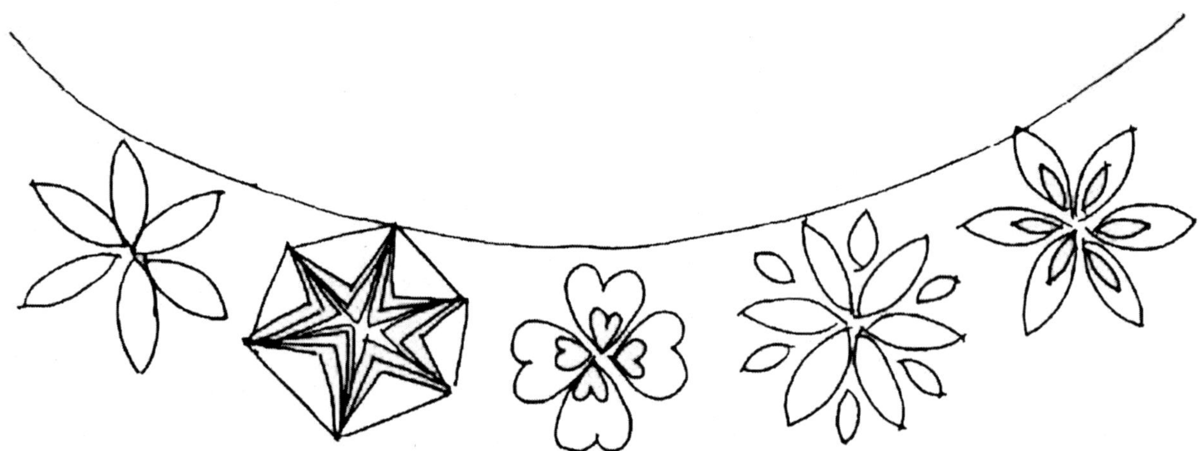

- Try a science experiment with salt crystal snowflakes. Dissolve as much salt as possible into hot water. Then, place your snowflake in a shallow tray. Carefully pour the salt water over your snowflake. Add just enough water to cover the snowflake. As the water evaporates, your snowflake will turn into a salt crystal!

- Create a snowflake design on a cake! Place your snowflake on top of a cake. Carefully and generously dust the cake with icing sugar. Your snowflake will be outlined in icing sugar on top of the cake!

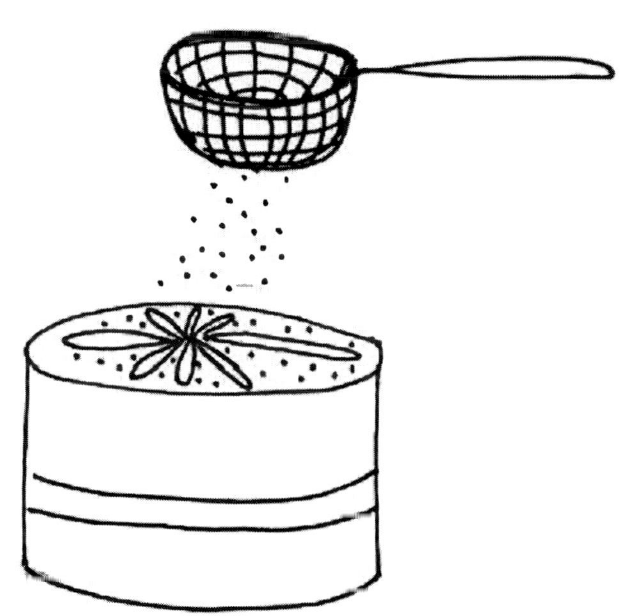

- Hang your snowflakes on a Christmas tree, mantle, or plant. Hanging snowflakes on a Christmas tree, an evergreen tree which is cut down and brought in the house during the Christian celebration of Christmas, is a traditional way to display snowflakes. If you don't have a Christmas tree, hanging snowflakes on the mantle, a shelf above the fireplace is another way to display snowflakes. If you don't have a mantle, try hanging snowflakes on houseplants, shelves or your walls.

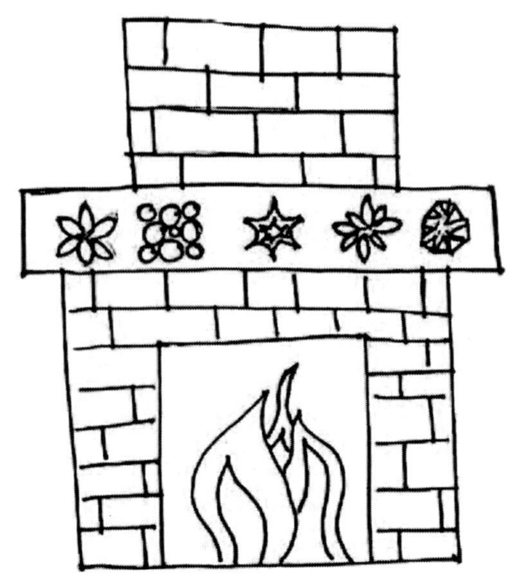

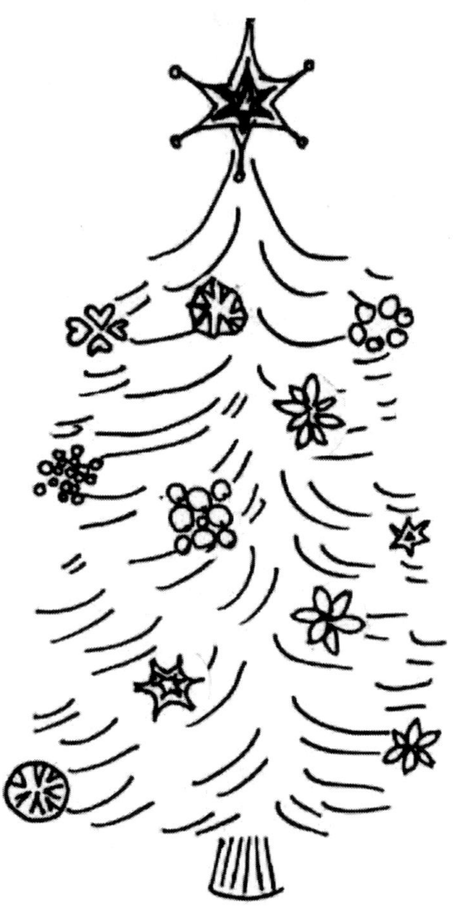

THE END

APPENDIX

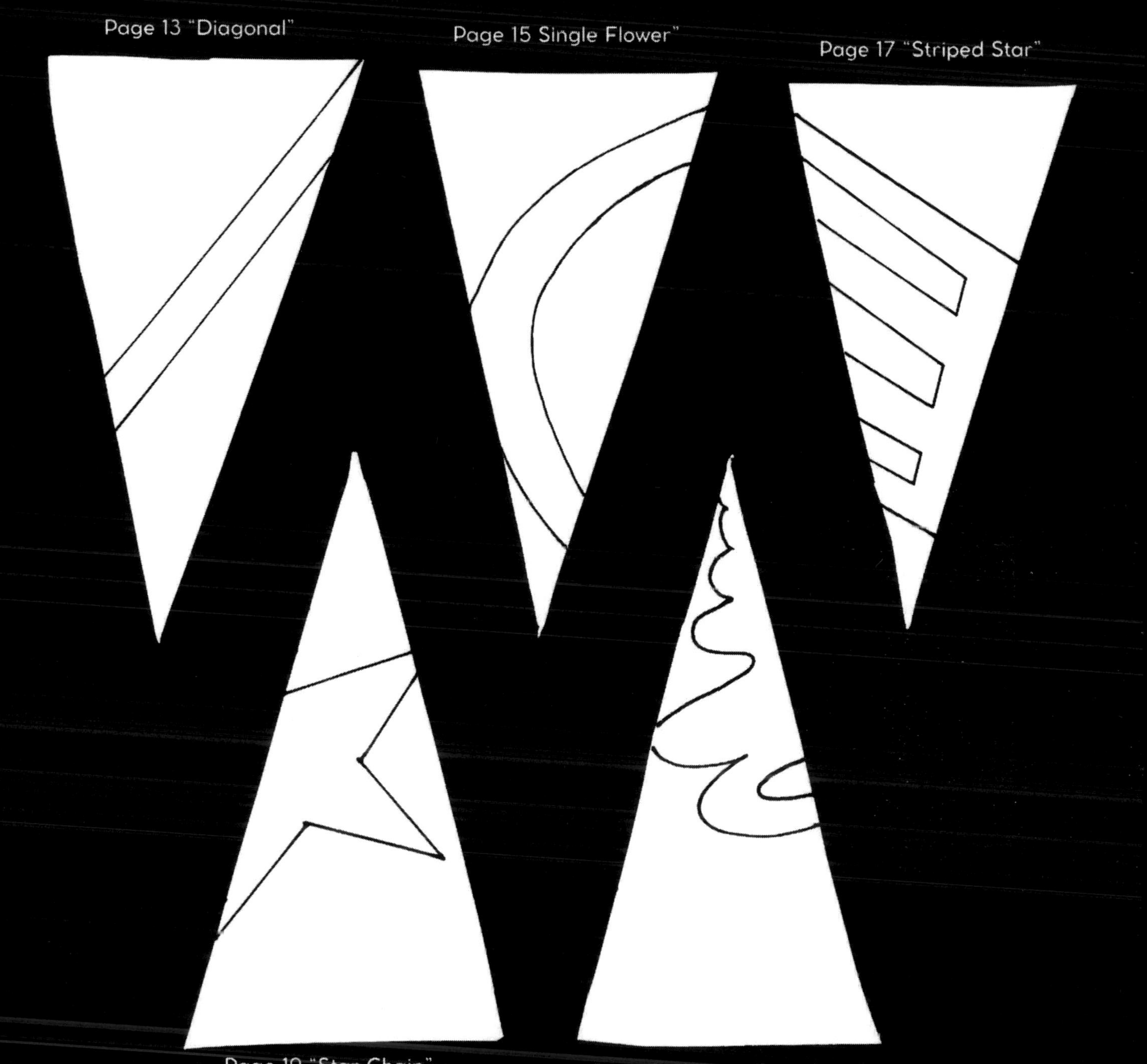
Page 13 "Diagonal"
Page 15 Single Flower"
Page 17 "Striped Star"
Page 19 "Star Chain"
Page 21 "Winter Snowflake"

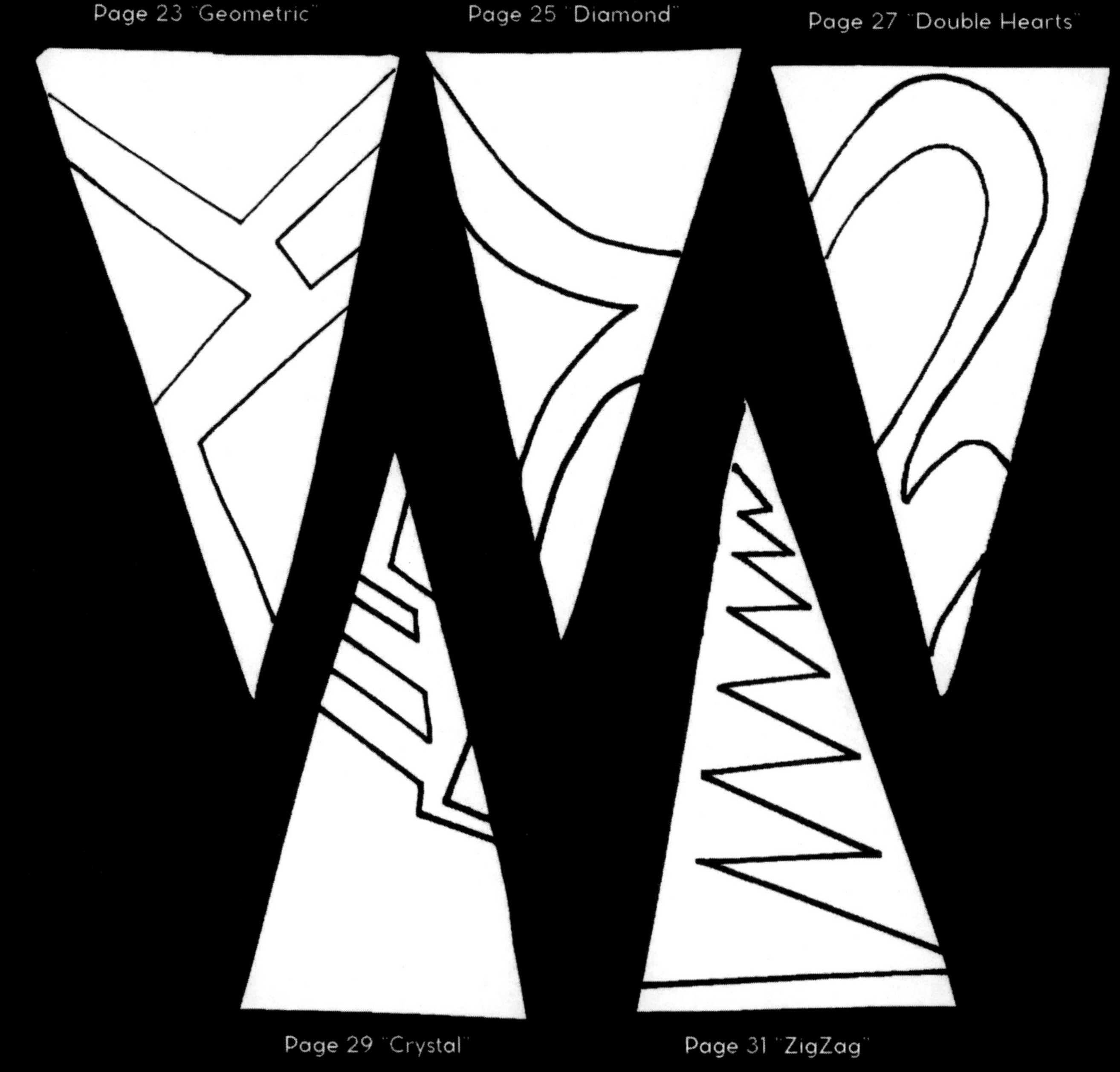
Page 23 "Geometric"
Page 25 "Diamond"
Page 27 "Double Hearts"
Page 29 "Crystal"
Page 31 "ZigZag"

Page 35 "Double Flower" Page 37 "Triple Flower" Page 33 "Hugable Heart"

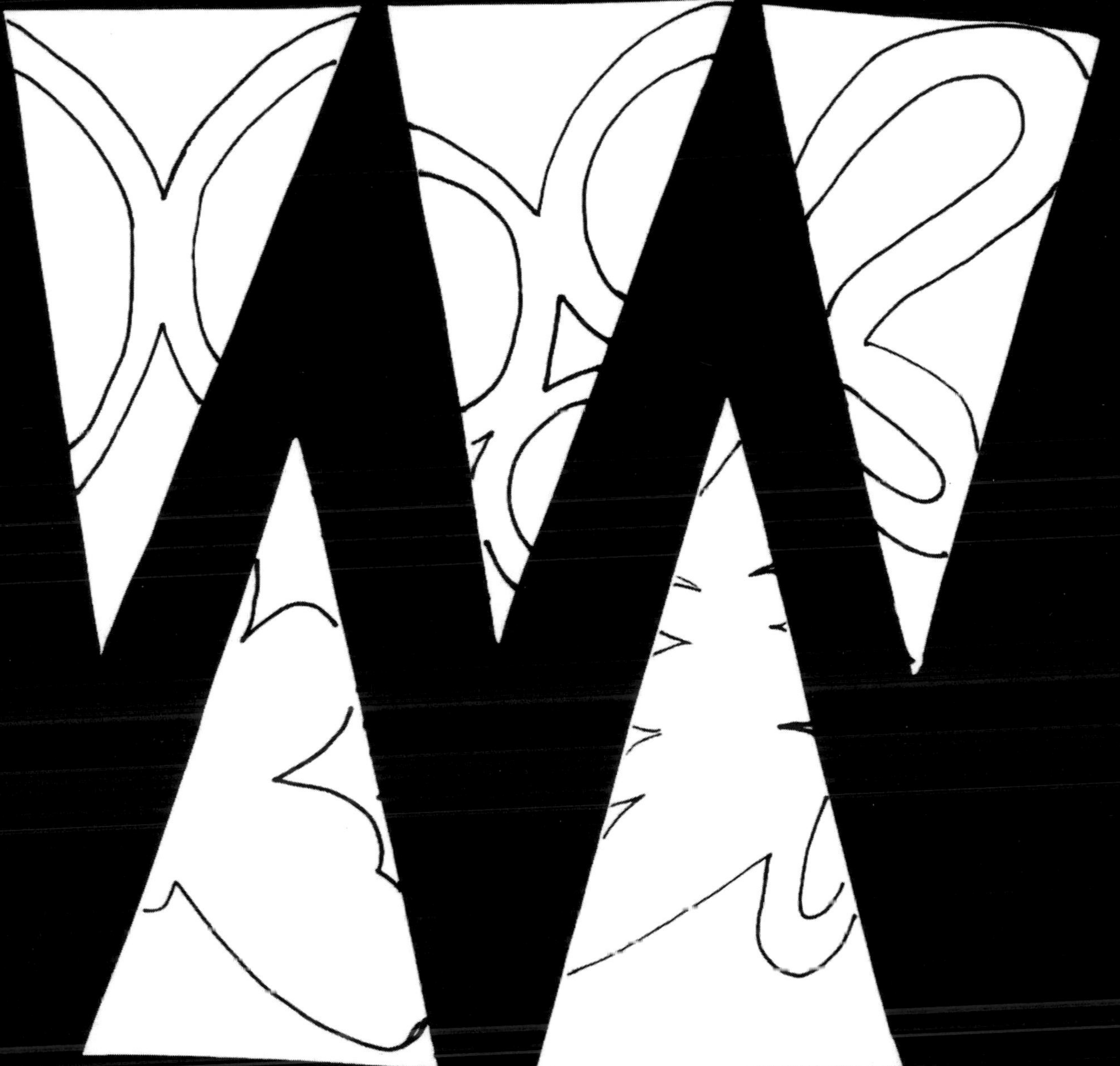

Page 39 "Butterfly" Page 41 "Swan"

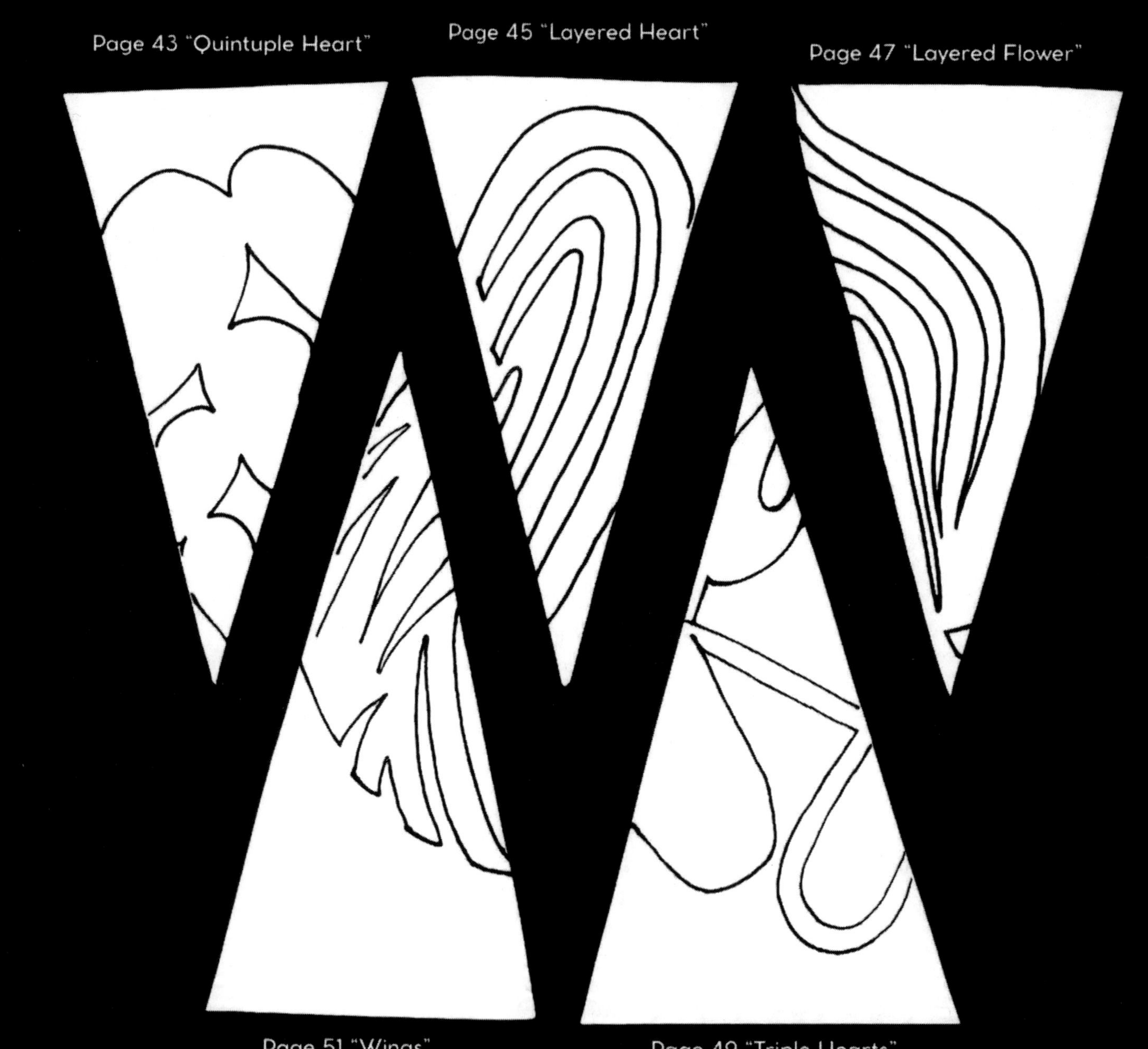
Page 43 "Quintuple Heart"
Page 45 "Layered Heart"
Page 47 "Layered Flower"
Page 51 "Wings"
Page 49 "Triple Hearts"

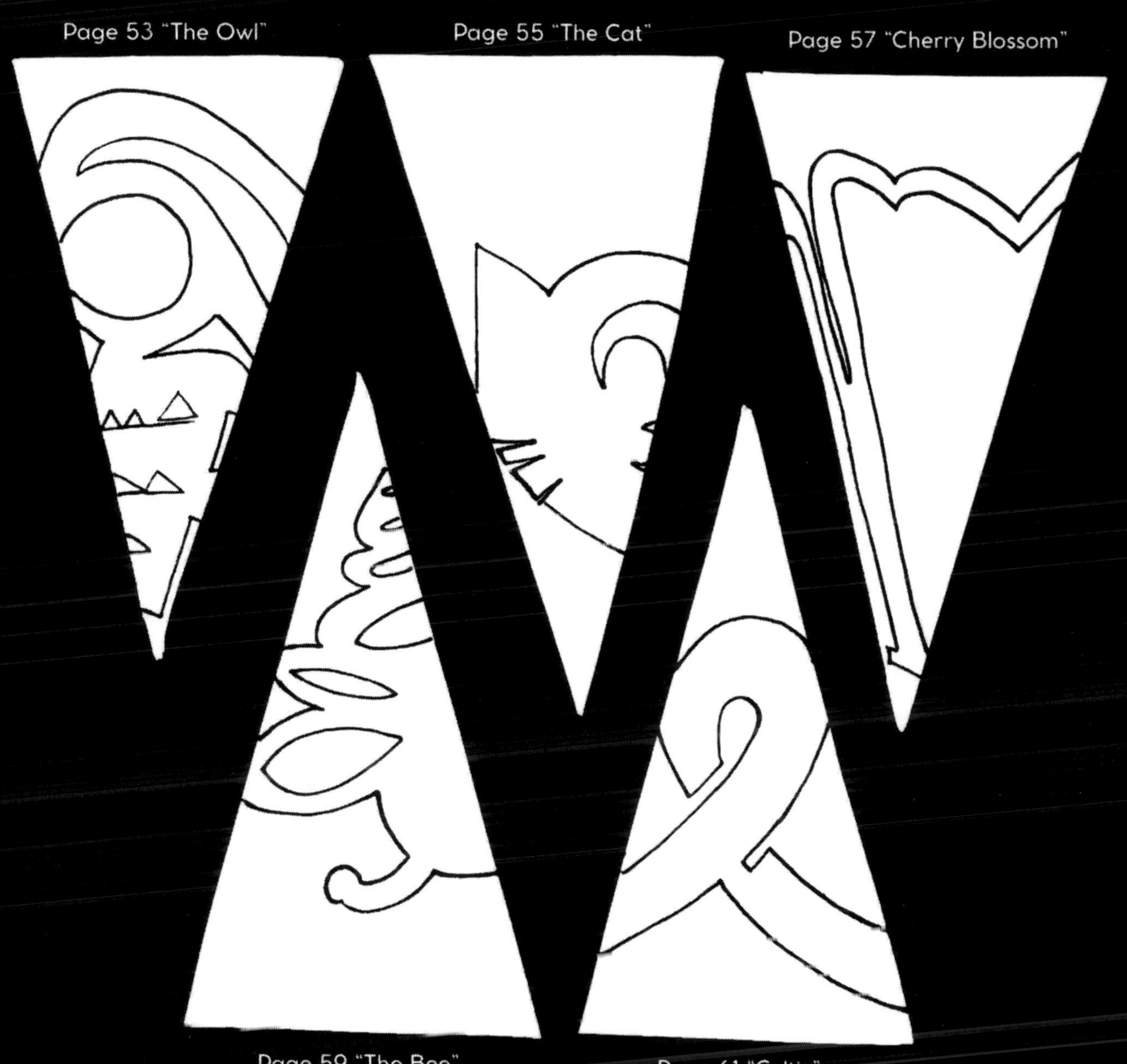
Page 53 "The Owl"
Page 55 "The Cat"
Page 57 "Cherry Blossom"
Page 59 "The Bee"
Page 61 "Celtic"

ABOUT THE AUTHOR

Ella Brett-Turner was born and raised in Toronto, Canada, where she made many messes cutting paper snowflakes in her parents' basement. Since then, she has earned a degree in Applied Mathematics from Brown University and moved to the snow-free Washington, DC, USA. In her spare time, she enjoys hiking, visiting museums, and making paper snowflakes.

Made in United States
North Haven, CT
01 January 2024